the

sacred art *of* slowing down

A. C. Seiple offers a profoundly holistic and compassionate approach to embodied soul care, guiding us through the sacred rhythms of slowing down, tuning in, and tending to the deepest parts of ourselves. With wisdom and grace, she weaves her own story and clinical expertise into a gentle yet powerful invitation—helping us recognize how our bodies and our souls are intricately connected and deeply worthy of care. *The Sacred Art of Slowing Down* is a beautiful gift for all who long to find healing, wholeness, and a deeper sense of belonging within themselves.

DR. ALISON COOK, host of *The Best of You* podcast, author of *I Shouldn't Feel This Way*, and coauthor of *Boundaries for Your Soul*

In a world that glorifies speed and productivity, *The Sacred Art of Slowing Down* offers sanctuary for those yearning to discover peace and cultivate resilience. By exploring embodied healing through the lens of faith, A. C. Seiple teaches you to connect with the aspects of your soul needing focused attention. Through practical wisdom and guided exercises, this book gently invites you to pause and listen to the depths of your inner being, welcoming the tender parts within. The author's attunement to her own story helped me understand mine in new and powerful ways. I believe the comforting guidance in these pages will also resonate with you on your journey of practicing compassion toward yourself and others.

KIMBERLY MILLER, MTH, LMFT, certified Internal Family Systems therapist and coauthor of *Boundaries for Your Soul*

In a world filled with overwhelm and trauma, it can be difficult to know how to engage the pain that keeps us stuck. *The Sacred Art of Slowing Down* is a timely and compassionate invitation to nurture and attend to, not only our wounds, but also our wholeness. A. C. Seiple is a wise guide for the journey—and this book is a powerful companion for anyone on a healing path.

AUNDI KOLBER, MA, LPC, therapist and author of *Try Softer* and *Strong like Water*

A. C. SEIPLE, MA, LCMHC

the sacred art *of* slowing down

Find Relief from Rushed Living, Soothe Your Soul, and Restore Wholeness Within

TYNDALE
REFRESH®
Think Well. Live Well. Be Well.

Visit Tyndale online at tyndale.com.

Tyndale, Tyndale's quill logo, *Tyndale Refresh*, and the Tyndale Refresh logo are registered trademarks of Tyndale House Ministries. Tyndale Refresh is a nonfiction imprint of Tyndale House Publishers, Carol Stream, Illinois.

The Sacred Art of Slowing Down: Find Relief from Rushed Living, Soothe Your Soul, and Restore Wholeness Within

Cover and interior photograph of landscape painting by Louis Patru (1895 - 1905), courtesy of Rijksmuseum, Amsterdam.

Cover design by A. C. Seiple and Libby Dykstra

Interior design by Laura Cruise

For information about special discounts for bulk purchases, please contact Tyndale House Publishers at csresponse@tyndale.com, or call 1-855-277-9400.

Library of Congress Cataloging-in-Publication Data

A catalog record for this book is available from the Library of Congress.

ISBN 979-8-4005-0632-1

Printed in the United States of America

31 30 29 28 27 26 25
7 6 5 4 3 2 1

To my clients

Who have taught me
more about being human
than any textbook ever could

contents

ADDITIONAL RESOURCES

foreword

I like to think of the long-term care of tending to the depths of our souls as tending to a garden.

A. C. SEIPLE

A. C. has become a treasured friend, not least because we share a common passion.

We're passionate about the exquisite intersections of Scripture and spirituality, and we're enlivened in our exploration of the dance between theology and therapy.

What I admire so much about A. C. is that with the grace of a dancer moving between light and shadow, she steps effortlessly between Scripture and silence, between theology's depths and the soul's tender wounds, weaving contemplation and therapy into a single, sacred rhythm.

Ironically, the sacred rhythm she commends begins with slowing down.

Slowing down. Did you hear that?

Sometimes it's hard when everything around you seems to be crying out, "You've got to do more, to be more!" Sometimes it's hard when even the books that are supposed to help simply apply more pressure, making demands of you that feel exhausting.

No, friends, this isn't one of those books that will try to convince you to exert more effort to get the results you want. Those are a dime a dozen on the self-help bookshelves.

Instead, A. C.'s invitation—seen in the three movements of her book—is to *slow down*, *tune in*, and *tend to*. Tune in and tend to what? *The lavish garden that is your own deepest being.*

Perhaps that lovely metaphor rings a bell. Five hundred years ago, another extraordinary woman reflected on the human soul as a garden that brings God great joy. St. Teresa of Ávila was a reformer in a day when religion had become ritualized; when life in God had become dull, dour, and dutiful; when powerful priests and bullying bishops were more interested in conquering and colonizing than in cultivating the garden of the soul.

Even amidst her own traumatic story, Teresa wrote a deeply personal work, *The Interior Castle*, which offers a revolutionary and healing invitation: God is at the very center of your being, offering you an opportunity to venture within, into a land of goodness and grounding, rest and refreshment. Her book, which she started writing all the way back in 1577, would be such a profound and lasting work of transformation and hope that the Catholic Church would recognize Teresa as the first-ever female "Doctor of the Church."

Today, Teresa's ancient vision of tending to the "garden in which the Beloved takes great delight"[1] is embodied in A. C.'s exceptional work. Perhaps the highest compliment I can give A. C. is that she is our Teresa for today. She is a physician of the soul, a gentle guide into the most sublime secrets of human flourishing.

A. C.'s garden-tending vision is not limited to the soul, however, but extends to psyche, soma, and story. As she writes, her book is a call to discover:

- the cognitive strands of our mind: our thinking patterns and the assumptions we hold, along with the ways these shape our perspective of the world around us;
- the somatic strands of our body: our bodily sensations and states, all the way down to the autonomic nervous system that is always running beneath our conscious awareness;
- the spiritual strands of our soul: the dynamics in our relationship with God, the different spiritual seasons we walk through, and the state of our soul; and

- the narrative strands of our story: the stages of development and events we have lived through that have shaped us, including the ways we carry the past with us in the present.

A. C. wants to see you flourish at your depths, in every facet of your being.

"Every facet of your entire embodied being is sacred," A. C. writes, "no matter how any of those strands has been forgotten or dismissed."

Everything is sacred. Every facet.

Can you imagine it? I know, it's hard.

The wounds within sometimes feel like they run deeper than anything else. The ache never quite abates. Sometimes we wonder if there is anything good within. Anything worthy. Anything redeemable.

In moments like this, we need prophets like St. Teresa, who see more deeply than we do. We need prophets like Jeremiah, whose ancient invitation was for a weary and wandering people longing for rest long, long ago: "Stand at the crossroads and look; ask for the ancient paths, ask where the good way is, and walk in it, and you will" (Jeremiah 6:16).

And we need a prophet like A. C., who sees you and me at our depths, bearing witness to profound goodness, calling us to courageous hope.

Dear reader, take a chance on the possibility that you really are a garden in which God takes great delight. And take this journey of slowing down, tuning in, and tending to guided by a woman of profound wisdom, whose roots run deep.

Chuck DeGroat, PhD, LPC
Grand Rapids, Michigan
February 2025

before you begin

For most of my life, I went about my days rushing around on autopilot. And this seemed to work just fine, apart from the fact that it didn't.

I wanted to get rid of the nearly constant current of anxiety I felt inside, but no matter what I did, it always seemed to come back. *Why didn't this knot in my gut catch the hint that it wasn't welcome here?*

I longed to find restful spaces to balance out the always-hurried and ever-busy days I pushed through. But even when I did slow down to rest, my mind kept moving a mile a minute. *Why couldn't I calm my thoughts and press into peace?*

I hated the person I became when I'd get caught up in blind frustration or defensiveness. I wanted to handle conflict differently, but under enough pressure, I always seemed to break. *Who was this version of me who would take over under stress?*

No matter how hard I tried not to be bothered by the noise in my internal world, something inside seemed to be perpetually causing problems. There was some sort of disconnect between the person I wanted to be and what stirred within, and rushing around on autopilot wasn't helping me bridge the two. Frustrated with myself, I'd wonder what was wrong with me. *Did I need to just pray harder? Put mind over matter? Get more therapy to do a better job changing my thoughts?*

Whether it's been explicit or unspoken, many of us have been taught to tune out feedback from our body, emotions that don't feel good, and the parts of ourselves we believe complicate our life—the facets inside that can feel like they're working against us.

Maybe we wish we could simply feel our feelings less, especially those that make us uncomfortable, but no matter what we do, we can't silence them.

Maybe we're sick of living in fear and want to live more boldly, but our feet seem to be frozen, unable to move us where we want to go.

Maybe we keep trying to grow in our faith, but any mention of God prompts a surge of anxiety inside, leaving us swirling in shame.

In these ways—and so many more—what stirs beneath the surface can all too easily feel like a problem, like something to tune out or get rid of.

But what if I told you that what's happening inside of us isn't necessarily trying to complicate our life? And what if the peace, healing, and change we most long for might come not from tuning out what feels like problematic noise but, instead, from slowing down and listening in?

When we've been conditioned to ignore what's stirring beneath the surface, we've also often been taught to prioritize the functioning of our thinking brain—reducing ourselves to just one sliver of who we are.

Here's the thing though: *We are so much more than our thinking brain.*[1] We are a multifaceted tapestry of heart, mind, body, soul, and more—*all wrapped up together in one unified and embodied being*. And what stirs within has something to tell us, something to say. When we slow down and learn to tune in and tend toward what's happening inside, we can create connections between our thinking brain and all the other strands inside us. And once we start to connect with the entirety of our created being, we can begin to build bridges where there has been disconnection, waking up the whole of who we are to navigate life in new ways.

This is exactly what we're going to do in the chapters ahead. We'll play with slowing down, getting to know some of the strands of our being that we might not be as familiar with so we can work *with* what's happening inside us, rather than feeling like we're working *against* our own selves. We'll trace the depths of who we are—our heart, mind, body, soul, and more—not dividing ourselves into separate categories, but instead, unifying and anchoring within. And as we connect more deeply within, we'll explore how we might move differently through life in new kinds of wholehearted—and whole body—ways.

Notes on Therapy and Spirituality

As we explore our internal worlds with therapeutic concepts woven into each chapter, I've attempted to offer language that feels natural and relatable. Whether these clinical frameworks seem oversimplified or too technical at different points, I invite you to first get lost in the stories throughout each chapter, connecting with what resonates at a gut level rather than trying to memorize or make sense of clinical terminology at a head level.[2]

In case you're curious about how I'll integrate spirituality in this space, I want to let you know what you can expect. I come from a Judeo-Christian faith background and love that the term *psychology* comes from Greek words that mean the "study of the soul."[3] I understand the word *soul* to refer to a holistic sense of who we are, and I understand the depths of the soul as our innermost being—which often feels mysteriously intangible yet is intricately connected with the tangible whole of our embodied existence.[4]

As we consider how therapeutic concepts might help us tune in with and tend toward the depths of our being, I will occasionally reference body-centered language that is expressed by ancient voices in the Psalms. I know some readers will be excited to see Scripture integrated in this way, while others will be skeptical or possibly triggered by an interaction with the Bible. My hope is that our engagement with these ancient texts will feel different from what many of us have experienced before.

Rather than using Scripture to induce shame or prescribe what we should do, we'll look at language that names everything from overwhelm and distress to safety—specifically how this is experienced in the body—and openly expresses everything from frustration and disbelief to trust in God. This will create space for us to be exactly where we are, tending to all facets of ourselves, not just the spiritually shiny or have-it-all-together parts of us. As we do this, we will simply notice the psalmists' words, being curious to consider the ways they demonstrate a deep connection with all of the strands of their embodied existence.[5] We'll also consider how Scripture depicts God's compassion, along with the embodiment of this compassion in the person of Christ.

If any reference to words from the Bible is triggering—especially if this is related to experiences of spiritual harm or trauma—*please know this book is not intended to try to force you into any kind of religious "shoulds" or spiritual bypassing.* I have seen and experienced Scripture used to harm, and I personally know how deeply wounding this is. My heart is not to press on wounds in a way that does not yet feel safe or that feels overwhelming.[6] Take or leave what I share in whatever ways you need to. These pages offer you permission to be right where you are every step of the way.

An Invitation

And now, as you turn the page, I encourage you to take curiosity with you as you enter and exit the chapters ahead. This book will invite you to play with a gentle moving pace, holding space for you to be present with your internal world. As you start to slow down, tune in, and tend toward, let yourself curiously notice how the internal shifts you experience might intersect with the world around you. Internal work does not, and cannot, happen in a vacuum. My hope is that these pages will draw you into new and restorative movements that will extend beyond your reading and into your relationships and communities.

May this be a sacred space for every part of you to be seen, held, and nourished in new ways.

Curious and skeptical depths of you, you are welcome here.
Weary and lively depths of you, you are welcome here.
Hurting and hidden depths of you, you are welcome here.

Let's walk together.

Anna Christine Seiple

PART ONE

slow down

CHAPTER 1

slowing down to anchor in

"Your body doesn't know that you're safe."

My therapist's words jumped out at me as she sat calmly in the chair across from mine. Meredith's office was bright, filled with natural light from a window that overlooked delicate trees dancing in a breeze.

I had started meeting with Meredith after moving to a new city for graduate school. Each week we would sit together, diving deep into pain that was too much for me to hold alone. In this season, my life felt fragile. More accurately, I felt fragile. Life as I knew it had been unexpectedly shattered a year before the move, and I was still picking up the pieces, trying to rebuild what felt like a mess of rubble around me. Week in and week out, this therapy office was a refuge, a place where I could process and sort out the sticky knots that felt tangled up in my mind.

On this particular day, I was feeling frustrated and stuck. There was some sort of disconnect inside of me that I could not resolve. On the surface, everything in my life seemed fine: I was blissfully dating my future husband, falling deeply in love with his big blue eyes and his tender heart. Beneath the surface, though, I was struggling not to feel consumed by anxiety. There was an unsettledness in my gut that would plunge me into fear or overwhelm in moments that felt both random and specific, moments when I couldn't think my way out of what I was feeling.

As the tension in my body lifted my stiff shoulders higher, my hands gestured in frustration. I looked at Meredith and said, "I *know* I am not in the past, I *know* this is different. I *know* I'm safe now and in a relationship with a different person. Why am I still getting triggered by every little thing? Why can't I just be calm and feel okay?"

Meredith knew my story and listened with unending empathy. I knew she wouldn't judge me as I exposed the confusion inside me that I didn't know how to make sense of. I expected her to trace the tangled thoughts in my mind, helping me make sense of their origins and why they were still creating problems. My goal was to leave her office feeling more settled in my thinking, with a clearer mind and a calmer headspace.

As she looked at me, I could see that she saw my confusion, frustration, and exhaustion. And even though I didn't understand it then, I now realize she was also seeing something else, something I didn't notice just yet. Instead of explaining psychological theories or trying to help me restructure my thoughts, she held space for the tension of my pain, reflecting back to me what she was seeing.

She spoke gently, saying, "It seems like your brain knows that things in your life are different now, but your body hasn't fully caught up yet. Your body still feels like you're *back there*, even though you're *here* now." Then she paused and calmly stated the words that jumped out at me: "Your body doesn't know that you're safe."

I'll be honest, my automatic reaction was, *What are you even talking about? That doesn't help me at all. Let's get back to the practical stuff so that you can help fix me!* Even though she was speaking English, it was like I was hearing her speak a foreign language. Normally I felt like our conversations were enveloped in the mutual understanding and safety we had cultivated in a year of therapeutic work together. Now, though, instead of feeling in sync, I sensed a disconnect—a disconnect from her words and a disconnect from my body.

For years before this day, my life had been permeated with spiritual disciplines that taught me to focus on everything *but* my body—prioritizing my thinking brain and behavior instead. In this mindset, my body was simply a means to an end for good words and spiritual disciplines. I wanted to walk closely with God, taking the counsel I was given for my faith seriously, longing for tastes of Eden, the green pastures of Psalm 23, and the warmth of Christ's compassion. And so based on the guidance I received, my brain and behavior became central to my life and my experience of being human.

I read my Bible daily and wrote in my prayer journal. I enjoyed reading through commentaries and Bible studies to learn more about the words I was devouring. I wrote Scripture on note cards and placed them around my house to remind myself of the truth whenever my emotions might tempt my brain to doubt. The way I was encouraged to practice these disciplines taught me to disconnect almost entirely from my body.

When my body was acknowledged, the most common message I received was that it was the epicenter of my sinful nature—what I was told was the core of who I was as a person. Similarly, I was frequently reminded that my heart was deceitful and sick, making emotions dangerous and untrustworthy. And so I tried as hard as I could to take control of my thoughts and behavior, attempting to force myself away from "negative" emotions and move toward what I believed was most good and true—right thinking and right behavior, which was a demonstration of a heart right with God.

As far as I knew, and as hard as I could try, I was doing everything "right," but still, I felt stuck. Something in the formula I'd been taught wasn't adding up—*there was some sort of disconnect.* And even though Taylor's now infamous words weren't written yet, I was asking myself if the problem was me.

Why couldn't I get it together? Why did something inside me respond in fear or overwhelm when I was supposed to be resting in perfect peace? I was exhausted from riding this loop over and over. I wanted to get unstuck, but I would have absolutely never thought that the relief I was longing for might come from connecting with what was stirring beneath the surface—what was happening in my body.

So when Meredith reflected that my body didn't know I was safe, it felt as bizarre and irrelevant as telling me that the rug on the floor preferred classical music over country. Honestly, it felt made up, a little too "out there" for my comfort. I had no category for talking about my body—or any other person's body—*knowing* or *not knowing* something. What in the world was she talking about?

I wanted Meredith to help me find a solution to what I saw as my biggest problem: *How can I get out of this emotion that I don't want to be feeling?* I didn't realize that she could clearly see the actual problem in front of me: I was out of touch with what was happening inside me, which was precisely why I was experiencing an uncomfortable disconnect between my thinking brain and what was happening in my body.

Mending a Disconnect

I'm curious if you can resonate with not being able to think yourself out of certain emotions, or feeling as though something inside is working against you. Maybe you've also experienced thoughts that won't go away, even when you ignore them. Or maybe you've also felt disconnected from your body or have been encouraged to stay detached from what's happening inside you.

In whatever ways my words might resonate with you, I'd love to share the journey I've walked since that day when I couldn't yet connect with Meredith's words.

This road has taught me that the formation of our souls runs much deeper than our thoughts and behavior alone—that *we are so much more than our thinking brain, and we were created for so much more than rushing—and reacting—through life on autopilot.* And before you wonder if I'm just expressing my opinion, let me share a nerdy fun fact with you. Don't worry, I promise I'll only nerd out for a minute here!

It's easy to go about our lives thinking that our brain is in charge of things, directing our body to take us where we want to go and to complete certain tasks. And while our brain certainly does send signals to our body, there's also a lot of communication sent in the opposite direction.

In fact, 80 percent of communication through our vagus nerve—a significant cranial nerve that extends from our brain stem to our chest and abdomen—flows from the bottom up, body to brain. Said more simply, 80 percent of these signals are sent from our body to our brain, rather than the other way around.[1]

In addition to regulating critical functions like our heart rate and breathing, the systems this nerve relates to are connected to everything from the interactions we have with other people, to how we experience stress, to how free we feel to relax and enjoy life—so basically, all the things. And rather than our brain solely dictating what's happening beneath the surface as we move through everyday life, most of this internal communication starts with our body, which sends signals to our brain.

So, while we might assume that our thinking brain is fully in charge of things, that's just not how we were created.[2] And if we want to cultivate holistic growth and formation in our life, working *with* this flow of internal communication—*with* the way we were created—is not only crucial, it is necessary. That's what this book is about, slowing down to tap into that 80 percent of communication that is sent from the body to the brain so we can work with what's happening inside, rather than rushing and reacting through life on autopilot in ways that can leave us feeling disconnected and frustrated. As we connect with all that's stirring within, we'll explore how this can wake us up to move through life in new ways.

Rather than seeing this as something we need to learn to do, I'd like to suggest it's something we've actually always known how to do—the world around us just makes it all too easy to fall out of touch with what's happening inside. I've seen this play out in front of me more times than I can count in the years that I've devoted to being a therapist. Time and time again I've savored helping people remember and reconnect with facets of themselves they've been disconnected from, so they can move through life in freer, more wholehearted—and whole-bodied—ways.

And more than being a therapist, I'm simply a person who only knows what I will share here as intimately as I do because none of this is solely theory or clinical concepts to me. What we'll explore in the pages ahead has intersected with my life in real and tangible ways that have genuinely changed how I move through my own days.

In the yearslong path I've been walking—and continue to walk—countless experiences and encounters with others have stitched together three key elements that will shape our movements here:

Slowing down
Tuning in with the body
Tending to the depths of the soul

While chapters in a book follow a linear path, our journey won't follow a three-step process to go from point A to point B. Instead, we'll walk through stories and play with new movements, taking our time to chew on and trace things we're often too busy to notice. More than a "how-to" that guides you through a specific kind of spiritual formation or therapeutic approach, this book encourages you to take a step back and connect within *before* trying to do any spiritual or therapeutic work. The invitation in these pages is to get comfortable with *being* before getting caught up in *doing*. You can think of the chapters ahead as a mosaic of therapeutic perspectives and contemplative reflections that hold opportunities for you to get out of your head and into your body, anchoring in the whole of who you are. We'll begin by getting curious about what happens when we slow down and create space to tune in with our body—along with the ways this can feel uncomfortable, risky, and even unappealing! As we play with slowing down and tuning in with what's happening inside, we'll explore the world beneath our thinking brain, peeking in to tend to the depths of our soul that might otherwise be forgotten. With every step, we'll move slowly and cautiously, not bulldozing our way to the depths of us, respecting that much of our internal world is often heavily guarded, and for good reason.

Now, I know that an invitation to connect with what's happening inside isn't always an exciting one. Sometimes it feels overwhelming or risky to really tap into what's happening beneath the surface, things we're keeping there for a reason! Sometimes it simply isn't on the schedule, and we wonder if our life has margin to open up an emotional construction zone. Or maybe it's just foreign, and we're not sold on the idea that this kind of thing is for us. Wherever you are, I invite you to walk with me, one slow, small step at a time, knowing that you can set your own pace along the way.

Woven Together

As we explore the mysterious complexity of our internal world, we'll get in touch with different strands that make up the whole of who we are. While I hesitate to try to define something so wonderfully mysterious into neat and tidy categories—and recognize that any language and categories we use will fail to perfectly express our internal world—I'll list some of these strands below to give you an idea of where we're going. We will explore how each of these is woven together in the fabric of our embodied being, oftentimes in ways we easily tune out as we go about our days.

- The cognitive strands of our mind: our thinking patterns and the assumptions we hold, along with the ways these shape our perspective of the world around us
- The emotional strands of our heart: the ways that we feel and are moved by emotions—both comfortable and uncomfortable—including the emotions we do and don't believe we have permission to feel
- The somatic strands of our body: our bodily sensations and states, all the way down to the autonomic nervous system that is always running beneath our conscious awareness
- The spiritual strands of our soul: the dynamics in our relationship with God, the different spiritual seasons we walk through, and the state of our soul

- The narrative strands of our story: the stages of development and events we have lived through that have shaped us, including the ways we carry the past with us in the present

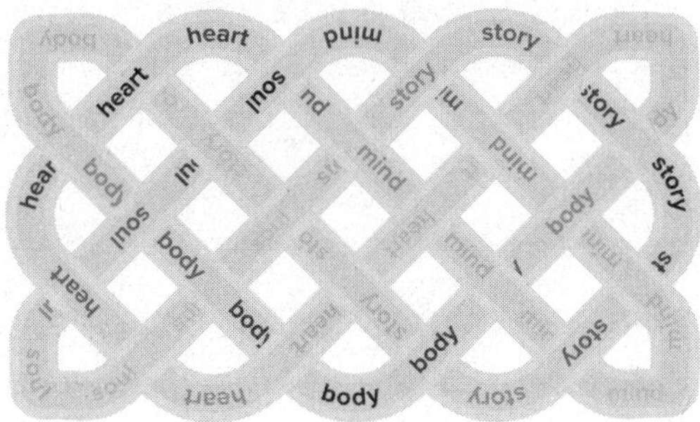

This list is certainly not comprehensive and simply represents one way to observe our multifaceted nature with everyday language that we often use to speak about different facets of our internal world. To help us tune in with these strands, and the ways they are connected to each other, we'll use *parts* language. When I talk about parts of us, I use terms such as *parts*, *facets*, *depths of the soul*, and *strands of our being* interchangeably.[3] It's important to note that when I specify a certain part or depth of us, I never use this language to indicate an internal division that separates any facet of us from connection to our whole. Instead, we will restoratively trace the fullness of our embodied being, within which all parts of us are already intertwined together, whether we realize it or not.

More than a piece of our personality or a mindset alone, I understand parts of us to be woven together in and through the strands listed above. I like to think about the image of a tapestry to explore the *both-and* of these distinct facets that are attached together in one whole.

A tapestry is one unified entity, with many different strands that are all connected together, even though this can't clearly be seen on the surface. In one corner of a tapestry, a specific thread, or a combination of two or three threads, might be most visible. In another corner, other threads might be more easily seen, possibly weaving together an entirely different picture. Still, beneath the surface, all the threads are interlaced together into one, with all of them contributing to the tapestry as a whole.

If you cut off or try to remove one thread, the tapestry cannot stay intact. The rest of the threads, along with the whole, will be affected. In these pages, rather than jumping to get rid of seemingly problematic threads of our being, we'll consider whether these strands might actually be part of the whole that was created in God's image—threads that don't need to be cut off, but instead, need tending and care. In this way, we will orient ourselves to restorative work that honors the whole of who we are, rather than taking ourselves apart in ways we were never meant to be unraveled.[4]

Think of a stressed-out version of a person who feels anxiety tightening their shoulders or chest, along with emotions of worry, fast-moving thoughts, and fears based on memories of the past that pop up in the present. And along with each of these threads, maybe they find it difficult to pray or feel settled in their faith. They might view what's happening inside as problems that are complicating their faith or ability to make decisions, like parts of themselves they'd like to get rid of.

Trying to silence or remove what they're experiencing inside might seem to be a helpful idea, but it would likely only be as effective as cutting off the tops of plants while their root systems are still anchored beneath the surface. What I am instead suggesting here is that tuning in with what's stirring within would be most helpful so they can tend to the many threads that seem to be causing problems—which are facets of their being that are actually in need of attunement and tender care.

Rather than trying to chop themselves up to feel less—which will likely only leave them feeling fragmented or defeated when the same problems return—they can instead explore restorative care, which honors the whole person God created. And that's where we're going: getting in touch with the many parts of our multifaceted being to cultivate a restorative wholeness within, one that creates space to engage with the world around us in new and wholehearted ways.

One reason I love using *parts* language to explore what's happening inside is because we naturally talk like this even if we haven't encountered formal parts work in therapy. We might say, "*Part* of me is really excited about my new job, but another *part* of me is nervous I'll somehow mess it up." We even have movies like the *Inside Out* films that depict *parts* of us as embodied characters, complete with storylines of internal conflict between emotions like joy, sadness, and anxiety.

And long before these movies were written, the ancient psalmists were using language that reflected the many strands within them. We can hear the raw emotions of these ancient poets as they simultaneously hold *parts* of themselves that are quick to sing in praise, *parts* of themselves that are flattened in lament, and *parts* of themselves that don't see God anywhere.

If parts language is new to you, I encourage you to be curious about how this concept sits with you. Simply notice what resonates at a gut level and what you don't feel so sure about. If you are familiar with this language but are used to a specific model of parts work that's different from my approach here, I encourage you to be curious about how your internal system responds to those distinctions.

As we trace different facets of ourselves, we will also consider how our life experiences and our wiring shape the ways that we move through life—how different parts of us can run on autopilot and react in specific ways. And even though we won't explicitly discuss concepts like neurodiversity, I want to invite you to be curious about how you are wired. Most simply, this is how you most naturally process information and navigate life in your brain and your body, rather than how you feel you *should* function when compared to some standard that has been set as a norm.

Our disposition can establish a baseline of sorts for what we experience as normal. Tangled up with this, certain thoughts, emotions, body sensations, and more can become normal to us on the other side of trauma, wounding relationships, and losses, desensitizing us to what life was like before, or what life could be like otherwise. Whatever you have walked through, and however your brain and body are wired, I honor you as you are and hope these pages are a safe place to explore a greater understanding of what happens inside you as you move through life. There is equal space here to consider the impact of past life experiences and your innate temperament—along with the interplay between these two.

Walking Together

I'm aware that talking about tuning in with the body and different *parts* of us might sound to you as it did to me on that day when Meredith could see that my body didn't know I was safe. It can be easy to scoff at suggestions to tune in with your embodied being as though it's some sort of tree-hugging jargon that's not for you. And while I do love trees, and have maybe been known to hug one or two, here's my invitation to you: *If you have a body, then you are indeed an embodied being, and this book is for you.*

It's okay if this feels risky and foreign like it did for me. It's okay if you are skeptical, wanting to hold what I share at arm's length at first. It's okay if you disagree with anything, taking only what fits for you and leaving the rest. There's space for different starting points and paths as we walk together here.

As you step into these pages with me, I want you to know that *I so wish I could be with you beyond these typed words.* While I wrote this book, one of the hardest things for me to sort out was how different it is to communicate with fixed words on a page rather than in dynamic and face-to-face communication that includes our entire embodied selves. I wish I could see your face and you could see mine, and that your body would know you are not alone as you travel through each sentence and paragraph.

And so, even if we have never met, please know that I have poured the attunement of my eyes, the warmth of my smile, the saltiness of my tears, and a full range of hand motions into these pages. On my back porch, in my home, and in countless coffee shops I have wept while writing these drafts, drawing from the most tender depths of my being to yours, hoping that maybe, just maybe, even if I can't be with you as you read these words, you can feel my presence with you in them.

Invitations to Pause & Play

One of the ways this book will invite you into a different pace is through the Pause & Play prompts that are sprinkled throughout. I've woven these prompts in to help us slow down, tune in with the body, and tend to the soul in experiential ways. As we'll discover, one of the most powerful ways to learn is through firsthand experience that helps us get out of our head and into our body. More than this, trying new things *with* another person is an even more effective way to create new connections—meaning, while these prompts can be explored alone, they will naturally resonate and stick differently if we explore them alongside another living and breathing person.

So, if you have anyone in your life who might be open to journeying alongside you, this is your cue to invite them to do so. Whether it's a friend, family member, small group, book club, or therapist, consider asking someone else to read through these chapters with you. More than conversation partners, they can be movement partners, walking with you through these chapters and the opportunities to Pause & Play.

Now, maybe you're planning just to skim the prompts and reflections you come across in these pages. If I'm being honest, I've done the same thing when I've wanted to get to the point in a book. In a way that's a bit different from traditional chapter formats, the Pause & Play sections are integral pieces of how each chapter is crafted—meaning there's no way to move through the book as a whole without them. So, even if it's literally for just sixty seconds, I encourage you to play with each of the prompts in this book.

Whatever time you have, be curious to notice *how* you interact with them. Notice what feels silly, what feels comforting, what feels uncomfortable, and what feels off-limits. And if all you sense is a disconnect, simply notice that. There's no need to try to force anything other than what naturally stirs within as you read through them.

If in your reflections you become aware of a spiritually anxious part of you that feels unsettled about connecting with your body and everything swirling inside, notice how it feels to gently remind yourself that God created all the facets of your being that you're tuning in with. We sometimes forget that the first words about our embodied being is that we were created in God's image and it was very good.[5]

If you feel overwhelmed by any words or prompts ahead, there is a detailed list of ways you can move with what's coming up inside at the end of this chapter. Those pages are there for you to bookmark and come back to at any point.

Lastly, while I hope that your experience of journeying through this book is therapeutic, it's important to say that this book is not a substitute for therapy or mental health services. If you notice that you are feeling distressed or overwhelmed by any thoughts and feelings that come up as you read, consider seeking a safe therapeutic space to process what you observe. PsychologyToday.com has an extensive directory of in-person and online therapists that can be filtered and searched through.

And now to begin, let's play!

PAUSE & PLAY:

INITIAL CONTACT

If it feels comfortable, place one hand over your heart and the other over your abdomen, taking a few deep breaths before continuing. If breathing deeply does not feel comfortable, don't force yourself to shift your cadence of breathing. If you prefer, explore placing your hands on your shoulders, neck, or legs as you take a few breaths, or simply hold your hands together. Any of these options is a simple way to start connecting with your body, helping you touch and feel the reality that you are an embodied being.

Without trying to analyze anything with your thinking brain or filter what comes out, notice what naturally pops up inside when you read over the following questions:

When I consider connecting with what's happening beneath my thinking brain in the depths of my soul, my gut reaction is ______

____.

The messages I've received about my body that most impact how I think about my body include ______________________,

________________, ________________, and ______________

____.

When I contemplate what slowing down might look like in the midst of my present life circumstances, I envision ______________ ____.

Take a breath and pause to consider what it was like to read through those questions. Did you like what came up inside? Did it feel embarrassing? Do you wish any of your answers were different?

Before moving on to the next chapter, read through the list below that provides ideas of how we can move with what's coming up inside rather than trying to escape it. As you continue to notice what's stirring inside, choose one option to play with before continuing on. See what it's like to feel what you're feeling, or think what you're thinking, while trying out one of the bulleted prompts below.

Moving *with* what's stirring inside[6]

- Go for a walk or stand barefoot on some carpet or grass. Wiggle your toes and let the soles of your feet play with the textures beneath them. Notice the sturdiness of the ground beneath you. If you'd like, place your hands on the ground, or consider lying flat on your back to simply breathe and be. Feel the sturdiness of the ground beneath your entire body. If it feels more comfortable, lie flat on your back with your legs resting up against a wall.
- Feel five different surfaces around you and notice their texture and temperature. For example, pay attention to the feel of the different fabrics of your clothing or the material of your shoes and jewelry. Touch a book, the ground, cold water, carpet, furniture, or a pet.
- Play with breathing at different speeds and volumes. Listen to how loudly or quietly you can breathe. Feel the difference it makes when you breathe quickly or slowly, allowing your body to settle into the cadence of breathing that feels most natural and anchored for you.
- Grab a journal or a piece of paper and draw or write whatever you are experiencing inside. Draw a comic strip that depicts what's

happening and moving inside you. See what it's like to externally express what's happening internally, whether it's with words, images, colors, or symbols.

- Standing up or lying down, stretch your body out as long as you possibly can. Then contract your body to bring your hands to your feet, allowing your fingertips to touch the tips of your toes. Next, watch your fingertips as they slowly move away from your toes, again extending your body as far as you can. Bring your fingers back to your toes, tracking this movement with your eyes.
- Imagine placing a pen in the hand of a part of you that's feeling strong emotions or wanting to cry out in some way. See what it's like to give this part of you a voice to express what they are feeling. Similarly, imagine writing or speaking to a part of you that's feeling strong emotions. You can do this by writing out dialogue, sketching stick figures and speech bubbles, or sitting across from an empty chair, engaging in a dialogue with this part of you.

CHAPTER 2

slowing down isn't so simple

I sat in the lobby, impatiently counting the minutes as they passed the top of the hour. I was waiting to begin my first spiritual direction appointment, unsure of what to expect. Friends of mine had worked with Shari, and they'd told me about the sweetness of slowing down with her and enjoying her direction, whether for an hour or on a silent retreat. Something in me was intrigued. Something else in me wasn't sold on it just yet. I was drowning in the details of a busy day, and I barely felt as though I had margin for this appointment. I wanted to make the most of the hour with Shari, but I also didn't want it to interfere with everything on the to-do list that was weighing on my mind.

Most days in this season were anything but slow and silent. I was in my third year of graduate school, moving through life with my thinking brain leading the charge. When I wasn't working on counseling coursework, I was spending my time on a second master's degree, digging into ancient languages. Day in and day out I worked my thinking brain overtime, weaving together coursework on counseling, ancient Near Eastern cultures, family systems, Second Temple Judaism, trauma, hermeneutics, couples therapy, and more.

Back then, moving slowly wasn't an option because I had more assignments to manage than was reasonable for any one person. When I would sit down to read or write a paper, I was always aware of the limited time I had as well as everything else I needed to get done. It was as if an internal gas pedal was always pressed to the max, trying to help propel me through the current stressor in order to get to the next task, over and over again.

And so as I waited for the hour of spiritual direction to start, I knew how many more minutes I had in my day and how much still had to be accomplished. And in that equation, I knew I had no time to spare. Fueled by an internal angst, I was trying to rush through an hour that was designed to slow me down. Not my best look, I know.

As seconds stretched to feel like hours, I watched Shari walk down the hallway with a warm smile on her face, inviting me to come back with her. Before she sat down, she calmly asked me if I'd like any tea. My mind jumped to do the math of how much time that might carve out of our hour together, time I didn't want to cut into. I tried to politely hide my instinct to hurry up and get started, attempting to embrace the cadence of the space.

Next, she unhurriedly pulled out a box of matches from her desk drawer, pausing with intentionality to strike the match against the side of the box and light a candle, all part of her process to invite us to hold silence together. I could see her delight in every step of this ritual. From the joy in her eyes and her calm presence, it was clear she was savoring the prologue of what would come next. Before we'd even begun, she was inviting me to slow down.

Now if I'm honest, the unhurried pace of her movements agitated something inside of me. Whatever was pressing on my internal gas pedal felt at war with this slower pace, almost threatened by it. Some fear inside me was worried about what might happen if I really let myself slow down. Some part of me was thinking, *Let's hurry up and get going already!* Deep in my gut, I could feel this tension bumping up against her gentle invitation to ease my pace. Slowing down didn't feel good just yet.

Can't Stop, Won't Stop

Slowing down creates space to tune in with the body and tend to the soul. The problem is, for many of us, life is fast-paced, and we're not used to a slower-moving rhythm. Whether or not we want it to be true, our body often moves at the pace of the culture around us, one that doesn't allow breathing room but demands that we push through life, no matter the cost. In this rhythm where most of our days are go-go-go, it often feels much safer to do and perform, finding "rest" in *doing* a good job or *doing* the right behavior. When this is the tempo we have known down in our bones, slowing down can feel like driving backward on the wrong side of the road.

Practically, it can feel painfully inconvenient to slow down when our to-do list only seems to get longer. Even if we can force mind over matter and jump into a minute of deep breathing or a yoga class, these spaces don't always feel good in contrast with our busy and often distracted lives. The moment there is space to simply be, we might start to notice things happening inside that we'd prefer not to feel, making slowing down feel risky at a gut level.

Slowing down means we might need to *be* with and feel emotions that aren't initially comfortable to acknowledge. Slowing down means we might feel the weight of our thoughts, which can run a mile a minute, overwhelming us when we aren't distracted by busyness. Most simply, slowing down threatens the predictable pace our body is used to.

I say all of this to validate the ways that slowing down is not as simple as it may seem at first glance. In this space, we are going to explore what happens inside as we slow down, so that we can understand the day-to-day muscle memory that carries us through life—the reflexive rhythms that might push back against our attempts to slow down, keeping that unhurried tempo seemingly out of reach. Rather than viewing the roadblocks and disconnects that get in the way of slowing down as problems, we'll tune in with what's happening beneath the surface so that we can learn to move *with*, rather than *against*, our body.

As my first spiritual direction session so clearly demonstrates, learning to slow down was not the prettiest process in my own life. Alongside the new pace I explored with Shari, my training as a counselor invited and required me to learn to slow down in new ways, a process that pressed up against what felt comfortable and known in my body.[1] If I'm honest, for years, no matter how much my thinking brain knew about the benefits of a slower pace, my body struggled to get on board. It felt impossible to shift gears, as if there were an internal gas pedal and brake system inside of me that ran on autopilot, outside my control.

The roadblocks in front of me were not just what was happening in my body, but also my perspective—how I saw things. For most of my life, moving slowly or stopping had negative connotations. I was taught a distaste for inefficiency and laziness, and I linked those vices with moving through life more slowly and pausing to take breaks.

In my mind, there were two main gears available to move through life—going or stopping. One was good and the other was bad. Going and moving were, of course, good: I believed I could *do* more and be more productive when I was in motion. And if I was more productive, I was stewarding my time and talents well. In this equation, slowing down or stopping was bad since I would seemingly *do* less, or worse, might even become stuck if I fully stopped. To keep going meant I wouldn't lose momentum, which at some deep level was held as a priority over taking breaks to really pause and breathe.

As I charged through each day, my soul was weary, even tattered. But it was hard to find time to tend to my soul when life was so go-go-go—any respites were infrequent. Even when I could find time, my body didn't know how to gently decelerate or fully sink into a peaceful and stationary rest. If I had an hour or two to breathe, the angst inside was determined to press the gas back to full speed ahead. The tragic irony was that I was skeptical of and avoided the very thing I needed more of.

These roadblocks and disconnects kept me cycling in fatigue, but they were harbored far beneath my thinking brain. At this gut level, the place where the muscle memory of how I would navigate life was stored, I didn't really *know* there were more options than stop or go. I also didn't trust that choosing to slow down or stop could be *not* bad, or even beneficial.

Now my thinking brain would have affirmed that I could navigate tasks and everything I needed to get done in different ways and at different speeds. But beyond cognitively acknowledging that there were different gears to shift through in life, I was stuck in the muscle memory of how my body actually navigated life.

It was as though there was a core facet of myself sitting in an internal driver's seat, and she was used to placing a firm foot on the gas. This was the way my body knew how to move through life. The perspective this facet of me held was one of *can't stop, won't stop*, a worldview that was bumping against the slower pace that Shari invited me into in spiritual direction. This perspective was skeptical and distrustful of trying out a different tempo, especially one that was associated with stopping.

In case any part of you can relate to the resistance I felt in the midst of a busy life that demands we go-go-go, we're going to play with wading in some slower waters before charging on into the chapters ahead. Even though it can initially feel uncomfortable or boring, if we don't do this first, we won't have the spaciousness we need to notice what's happening beneath the surface. When we slow down, we create room to journey into new depths of curiosity and connection, necessary ingredients to tune in with the body and tend to the soul.

PAUSE & PLAY:

SLOWING DOWN

For just a few moments, I invite you to play with slowing down and observing what happens inside you.[2]

Before starting, place your hands over your heart, abdomen, or shoulders and take a couple of deep breaths. Gently remind yourself that there's no right or wrong way to sit and be for the minute. And if it doesn't feel possible to offer yourself this permission, imagine that I am gently offering this permission, reminding you that there's no correct or incorrect way to be still for this minute.

Now either set a timer on your phone or watch a clock for one minute. Rather than trying to be comfortable right away, allow yourself to be uncomfortable if that's where you are. See what it's like to notice if something inside you wants to press on a gas pedal or if you're enjoying pressing on the brakes for this minute. Give yourself complete freedom to notice any of the ways you don't like slowing down or anything inside that savors this slower moment. Remember that whatever you notice is neither right nor wrong.

At the end of the minute of silence and stillness, ask yourself the following questions:

How aware or unaware of my body did I seem to be during that minute?

What kinds of thoughts were popping into my mind? What was happening in my body in response to these thoughts—for example, did certain thoughts lead me to tense up or to take a deep breath?

Did I notice a resistance to slowing down? If so, what did that feel like in my body?

Did it feel soothing to slow down? If so, what did that feel like in my body?

If you have time in your day or week, consider extending this exercise to two or five minutes, noticing how the longer amounts of time open space to slow down more deeply. If any part of you feels panicked or overwhelmed by slowing like this, consider allowing yourself to take a walk or jump around for a few moments before or afterward.

This kind of movement helps our body move with and through anxiety and overwhelm. Offering ourselves space to move can also help all parts of us know that we're listening and not trying to rigidly force ourselves to do something that might not feel comfortable or safe enough to play with yet.

Must Stop

In spiritual direction with Shari, I was introduced to a new question: *What is the state of your soul?* I had never considered this before. Other than recounting the highs and lows of a week, I had not really explored my internal world in a spiritual space. It was easy to breeze by the lows, not wanting to stay too long in any discomfort, bypassing what was happening beneath my thinking brain and jumping into prayer requests or praise reports with the people around me. Brief highs and lows didn't require I feel the weight of my internal world for too long.

When I met with Shari, we always started our time holding silence. Then she would ask me this one simple question about the state of my soul, inviting me to slow down and create space to survey my internal landscape, the internal landscape that was all too easy to live disconnected from. When I paused to consider her question for even a moment, I'd be reminded that there was a fatigue and a heaviness weighing inside me that I didn't know what to do with in general, let alone in a spiritual space with ample time to feel its full weight.

And then just when I thought I might be learning to dip my toe into slower spaces, I felt as if a lightning bolt struck my life. Only fourteen months after we said "I do," my husband, Elijah, suffered a traumatic brain injury.

Before Elijah's accident, our lives were full of life and light. We'd become friends in seminary before we joined our lives together, spending our days working side by side, delighting in our shared love of learning and growing. Now our lives had become confined to a dark room, which we soon realized would be home not just for days or weeks, but months or maybe longer.

I felt helpless and crushed as I watched my best friend bear unspeakable and unceasing pain. I was also grieving the loss of friends who would not sit in the discomfort of the dark room with us, along with those who could not, feeling the distance of family and dear friends who lived far away. In the thick of what felt like an all-consuming grief, long-standing autoimmune issues that I thought I had learned to manage flared up worse than ever before. It felt like my existence, along with my sanity, was dissolving.

If I thought I didn't have time to slow down before his accident, I certainly didn't have time to slow down afterward. It didn't matter that my body was exhausted. I continued to press forward on the gas pedal inside of me, day in and day out, until one morning when I couldn't keep going any longer.

I remember waking up that day, barely able to open my eyes as I shuffled to the bathroom, nearly groaning after having hardly slept again. This was one of many sleepless nights that had been strung together after relentlessly heavy, anxiety-soaked days. That morning I no longer had any energy to push me forward. I stumbled about ten slow steps to the bathroom before I fell to the ground, collapsing in tears. What was happening inside me wasn't just an emotional response. I could feel that my tears were flowing from the core of my body, which no longer had anything left to give. I had never experienced my body physically giving out like this before, crumbling into a full stop.

My body had slammed on the brakes, completely fried from too much long-standing stress. Everything inside me wanted to cry out—but at the same time, I didn't have the strength to feel or express anything. This was a new kind of pain and loss, one that pierced the depths of my soul. It was all too much. My body was crying, *Stop!*

Shifting Gears

As someone who had lived most of her life resiliently pushing through pain and stress, I didn't see this change of pace as a helpful invitation to something new. Instead, it felt like one more problem to manage. More than this, it wasn't a pleasant experience. Rather than gently decelerating into a respite, I felt as if my body had been slammed to a stop in a crash, like a holistic whiplash.

What felt like the cherry on top of all this unloveliness was that as my body fell to the ground, crying, *Must stop!*, I didn't have a choice in slowing down or stopping. My body had made the decision for me.[3]

Because of my negative associations with slowing down, along with the reality that I didn't have margin to stop going in my current season, this was not just something new, but something unwelcome, something I viewed as bad.

At the time, it was terrifying for me to see that my body, not my thinking brain, might make decisions on my behalf. I was already in a vulnerable and fatigued space, so to feel as though my own body could seemingly work *against* me felt like a nightmare. What I hadn't considered was that maybe my body was trying to help me, and maybe there were ways I could help my body.

While we'll explore our internal gas pedal and brake system further in later chapters, for now, we'll keep it simple: Our autonomic nervous system is wired to flexibly move between being mobilized to *go* and immobilized to *stop*. And depending on the circumstances, when our body shifts gears to slow down or stop, we're either lulled into a secure sense of rest and safety, or we're pushed into a more disorienting halt.

As we move through these different cadences, we can learn to work *with* our body rather than feeling as if our body is working *against* us. And in order to do that, we need to first be connected to our body. Once we tune in with what's happening beneath the surface, we can begin to understand our current movements, along with what has shaped this muscle memory. Only then can we gently work with what stirs within, rather than hopelessly fighting against ourselves.

Like any other relationship, connection with our body takes time to build, and hurrying will leave us with unsteady foundations. When someone rushes through a coffee date or dinner with us, we don't tend to feel connected to them. When someone takes time to get to know us and regularly spends time with us, we know that we matter to them, and vice versa. It's the same with our body.

When we slow down to create time and space to connect with what's happening beneath the surface, even when it's uncomfortable—or perhaps especially when it's uncomfortable—we're investing in opportunities to foster a connection where there has been disconnection. And only when we start to repair this disconnect can we gain perspective on the depths of our being that may have been forgotten and neglected for years and even decades, parts of us that are often in need of tender care.

To invite the whole of our being to slow down is not just about a change in pace. It's also about recognizing the many facets of who we are, which run far beneath our thinking brain. All parts of us are so creatively knit together in our embodied existence and worth slowing down to get to know, connect with, and care for. In the next chapter, we'll explore how we might start to connect to our body in new ways, exploring the feedback we can be quick to tune out or dismiss. Before we turn the page, take a few moments to slow down with the prompts below.

PAUSE & PLAY:

INVITING A NEW PACE INTO YOUR DAY

Take a moment to notice how the idea of slowing down is sitting with you at a gut level. If it feels comfortable, place your hands over your heart or abdomen and ask your embodied being the following questions.

> *How do I feel about slowing down?*
>
> *Does it feel intriguing or refreshing? Would I use a different word to describe my internal reaction to slowing down?*
>
> *Is something inside skeptical or annoyed when I think about slowing down?*

Take a breath or two as you survey what's stirring internally, noticing whether there's a mixture of reactions.

Next, play with one way you can work *with* your body to slow down today.

- Maybe you can take an extra minute as you brush your teeth or wash your face to let your fingers and hands move more slowly, seeing what it's like to do these things at a totally different tempo than what's engrained in your muscle memory. Notice the sensations of water, toothpaste, or soap against your skin. What's something you notice in this moment that you normally wouldn't be aware of?

- Maybe you take a few extra minutes at a meal to chew your food more slowly, seeing what it's like to notice the muscles in your jaw as you chew. What's something that you notice in this moment that you normally wouldn't be aware of?
- Maybe you take a walk and see what it's like to move one foot in front of the other at half the speed you would normally move. What happens in your body as you intentionally move so slowly, seemingly so inefficiently? What's something you notice in this moment that you normally wouldn't be aware of?

CHAPTER 3

slowing down with our body

From the time I was a kid, I felt at war with my body. It didn't matter if I was in a dance class or sitting still, pain was a constant companion. The feedback my body gave me was uncomfortable, exhausting, and inconvenient. If I were aware of my body, I would have to feel the daily migraines throbbing in my head, the unceasing aching in my neck, and the never-ending fatigue that seemed to be everywhere all the time, whether or not I had gotten a full night of sleep.

For years, there was no respite or solution. Each day my body would scream in pain, and I would try to figure out how to turn down the volume or press the mute button. It was the only way I knew how to survive it.

By the time I was a young adult, I felt as if I had a part-time job as I balanced appointments with countless specialists and underwent various tests to try to figure out why my body seemed to be attacking me. Eventually, I learned that I was battling a number of autoimmune disorders and diseases, none of which came with helpful answers. And through it all, I looked normal and healthy on the outside, confusing people who assumed everything was fine.

I had become so skilled at tuning out pain that in my early twenties, when I felt new pain in my feet whenever I walked or danced, I assumed it was simply the aftermath of dancing as a child. I'd rationalize it away, thinking, *Most dancers eventually have foot pain later in life, and mine is just coming a bit early. Into the noise-canceling closet it goes!*

Eventually the pain became so severe that I went to the doctor. I was X-rayed, assuming the worst injury he might see would be a stress fracture. When the doctor joined me in the exam room, he placed my X-ray on the wall and pointed to the image. "Do you see this piece of bone here?" he asked. I looked and nodded, not sure what the bone should look like.

He added sternly, "Do you see how it's not connected to the rest of your foot?" I was stunned, barely able to respond with a soft, "Oh."

The doctor was more confused than I was. He couldn't understand how I'd lived with the pain for nine months before coming to see him. Those nine months included daily walks, weekly three-hour tap classes, and occasional jogs. He wanted me to heal so I could be active again, but he was concerned that my autoimmune issues might prevent me from healing properly after surgery.

And so, instead of a surgery date, I left that appointment with a bulky cast on my left foot and an oversized pair of paper shorts around my waist. Moral of the story, don't wear skinny jeans to an appointment where you might be put into a cast—the jeans will have to come off before the cast goes on and your only alternative wardrobe option might be paper pants.

Now what I hadn't told the doctor was that I was experiencing similar pain in my *right* foot, the one that would now bear a heavier load. In my defense, I hadn't been convinced that my foot pain was a sign that something was actually wrong, and my left foot hurt much worse than the right did. I had spent *years* without finding helpful answers for most of the pain my body carried, so the lesser pain in my right foot surely wasn't anything serious, right?

As I walked around with my left foot in a cast, I slowly started to tune in with the pain that I had previously tuned out. I began to recognize how the nuances of this pain differed from the pain I had lived with for years. And as I got to know *this* pain, I realized I also had a problem with my right foot. I had learned what fracture pain felt like in my left foot, and I knew this was what I also felt in my right foot. So back to the doctor I went, sheepishly suggesting another X-ray.

This time I wasn't surprised when he found a fracture in my right foot. The doctor's eyes got wide when he reviewed the X-ray with me, unable to believe that I had been walking, not just on one broken foot, but on two. Into a second cast I went, but this time I left wearing my own shorts, avoiding another run-in with their wardrobe of paper pants.

For years before this, I hadn't tuned in with my body for the simple reason that it didn't feel good. Once I was confined to two casts, I started to rethink my approach. Clearly, my discomfort was trying to tell me something. I had to wonder if my body had been informing me of the fractures for months. *If I had known how to listen to the pain, could my feet have healed sooner? And if my body had something important to communicate in this case, what other helpful information might my body be trying to tell me?*

Ancient Languages

Fast-forward to my training as a counselor, which taught me about the science behind our body keeping the score in life. In my thinking brain, I started to learn that what's happening in our body is inseparably connected to our emotional, relational, spiritual, and mental health.[1]

Still, no matter what facts I learned at a head level, I was hesitant to *really* trust or even value tuning in to what my body was trying to communicate. At the core of this struggle was my belief that connecting with the body might be incompatible with expressions of Judeo-Christian faith. Much of what I had learned in Christian spaces had taught me to believe that the body was just our flesh. And wasn't our flesh bad?

And then one day I noticed something in a psalm that started to shift my perspective. I had read these words before, but this time, I saw something in the lines I read, something I hadn't seen before. I was struck by the intimate connection between these ancient psalmists and their bodies. And as I read their words, I wondered if the whole body-connection thing I was learning as a counselor wasn't so separate from my faith tradition after all.

I used the tools I had learned in my biblical studies degree to uncover what these voices were saying, translating their ancient language into ours, assuming at first that this was the only translation work I was doing.

Instead of engaging with only an ancient written language, though, I soon realized I was working with another as well—a dialect that reached deeper than the thinking brain. These words were so clearly crying out from the depths of the soul, a kind of holistic and embodied language that the ancient Israelites were clearly fluent in. As I sat with these words, they slowed me down, showing me that I didn't need fancy translation tools to appreciate how deeply connected the psalmists were with what was happening in their body.

We don't need to know ancient Hebrew to connect with feeling like our heart is beating so violently that it's as though it's about to burst.[2] We don't need to take a class in ancient Near Eastern literature to relate to resting in such a sense of safety that everything in our body feels fully secure.[3] We don't need to travel back thousands of years to resonate with being so overwhelmed and numb that we've lost our appetite.[4] All we need to do to connect with these experiences is to slow down and be present with them. Our body *knows* these kinds of experiences at a gut level. And if we slow down as we consider these ancient words, we can see just how deeply the ancient Israelites were connected with this inner knowing.

The psalmists didn't limit their spirituality to their thinking brain or use their body solely as a means to an end as they engaged in spiritual disciplines. Instead, their messy and raw songs express the fullness of their embodied humanity in cries of sorrow and songs of joy. These were people who referred to the innermost depths of their internal world as their "kidneys and hearts"—words we often translate today as "minds and hearts" to match how we talk and think.[5] As we slow down with their words—and their holistic understanding of being human—we find countless invitations to explore a multifaceted connectedness in our internal world, one that doesn't separate body and mind or thoughts and emotions.

They don't hold back as they attempt to name what's happening inside, describing their heart as dead and withered grass.[6] Their words invite us to notice how we experience emotions in our body as they speak about their heart being like wax in distress, melting deep inside the body as their bones feel out of joint.[7] They can spur our curiosity to pay attention to what is happening inside as they cry out because their soul feels like it's falling apart and dissolving with their inner groans.[8]

They invite us to name the depth of our human experiences, likening themselves to a lonely bird out in desert spaces when feeling overwhelmed and weak. These writers didn't limit their faith or communication with God to their thinking brain or verbal language. Instead, they invite us to tune in with our heart's roaring.[9] Rather than dismissing internal growls as unintelligible or unimportant, as we might do, they listened—and also told God about it.

I can't help but read their words and wonder, what if our internal groans are intelligible, and we just don't know how to speak their language yet? Or maybe, and possibly more accurately, what if we were created *knowing* this kind of connection to our body, but we have just fallen out of touch with it? And if that's the case, what might it be like to remember and relearn this kind of holistic existence?

PAUSE & PLAY:

FEEDBACK

As we start to slow down and tune in with our body, identifying potential roadblocks can make the process feel less frustrating. Often, the obstacles getting in the way of connection with our body are informed by messages we received from other people.

I'm curious: What were you told about the feedback your body gives you? This might be related to what your body might have to say through pain, emotions, discomfort, or anything else.

To chew on this, take a few minutes to move through the questions below. Consider drawing stick figures with speech bubbles to represent the ways you learned how to listen to, or not listen to, your body. Or consider acting out situations where you received messages, implicitly or explicitly, about how to listen to or ignore your body.

You can act them out either by playing different parts of yourself, or simply by picking up toys or household items and using them to represent people having a conversation. Think about how little kids can pick up a rock and a stick and turn them into characters who are talking to each other. See what it's like to feel a little silly with one of these prompts as you explore the questions below.

Was I ever told to listen to my body? If so, how?

Was I ever told not *to listen to my body, or to ignore my body in any way?*

How did I see others around me tuning in with their body, listening to what their body might want to tell them?

In what ways did I see others tuning out and disconnecting from their body, ignoring what their body might have wanted to tell them?

Remembering What the Body Already Knows

When Jack entered my counseling office, I knew I was in for a treat. This little guy was full of energy, always thrilled to be in a therapy session and entirely chaotic in his enthusiasm. He was one of the youngest clients I had worked with, and he taught me new kinds of patience and play each week. He left me with some unforgettable memories, including a day when he simultaneously sneezed in my face and wet his pants. Needless to say, that was not my favorite day as a therapist.

When working with little ones like Jack, I always appreciated how different our therapy sessions looked from therapy with adults. I can still picture myself kneeling down to sit on the outdated carpet of my first counseling office to begin an art and play therapy session, positioning ourselves to have easier access to toys, sand, and artwork.

One Tuesday, Jack noticed a worksheet on my desk. It had an empty outline of a body with a simple key for emotions, prompting a person to color in where they felt those emotions in their body. When he saw the worksheet, he asked, "What's that?"

I held it up, slowly explaining, "This piece of paper helps you think about where you feel emotions, like being happy, sad, or mad, in your body. Each of the words down here is an emotion, and you get to choose a color for each one and then draw it in the body to show what that emotion feels like inside of you."

As I spoke, I wondered if he was too young to grasp the concept and would lose interest or simply scribble on the piece of paper, ignoring the prompt. Instead, he started to point to emotions, asking me to read the words he couldn't decipher yet. He sat still and without hesitation grabbed a specific color of marker for each emotion, not needing further prompting.

He first drew happiness as orange rays of sunshine radiating through the face, excitedly telling me what this felt like in his body as his own smile spread from ear to ear. He sketched anger as red lightning bolts charging the set of legs, kicking his feet as he told me how this felt with a frustrated tone. I sat there mesmerized, watching this tiny human teach me just how innately we are connected to our body, knowing how to speak about what was happening inside of him as though it were an inherent mother tongue.

And he wasn't the only child to teach me. The next week, another little one drew joy as pink smiley faces warming his heart, pulling me in to savor the sensation we feel inside when we're delighting in something that connects our heart with our face. The following day, I witnessed a little girl draw sadness as blue cats streaming from her eyes. Her face dropped as she drew these crying cats spilling out of the eyes, reaching all the way down the body. Alongside these cats, she sketched fear as green squiggly lines coursing through her hands and feet, shaking her body around to show me what this fear felt like inside.

Picture by picture, these children were educating me in just how intricately our experiences of emotions are woven into our body, well beyond the limitations of verbal language. These young ones let their shapes and squiggles speak, communicating with me at a gut level. The colors, shapes, and somatic nuances drew me into the felt sense of each emotion in my own body and to a felt sense of being human.

After Jack and the other little ones amazed me with their natural connection to their emotions and body, I started offering the worksheet to adults as well. Too often, rather than speaking this body language fluently, my adult clients seemed to have forgotten it almost entirely, not convinced that this was a language they had ever known. The moment they saw the worksheet, most would shrink back, saying things like, "I have no idea how to do that," or "I'm not good at that kind of thing."

If I would come alongside them, honoring and holding their concern, I'd watch them reconnect with a language they didn't even know they spoke—an inner ancient language that came alive in the room with us. I would then witness these clients connect with a sacred internal world. It was as if I was watching them honor the humanity that lived inside of them in a new way.

A father of teenagers effortlessly drew blue wells of sadness resting deep in his gut. We sat in silence to honor the grief no one had ever asked him about, grief that he listened to for the first time in that moment.

An anxious first-year teacher who felt panicked and helpless in her new job drew abrasively, sketching pink and red fear surging through her chest. Before this, she had been holding this fear alone, feeling as if she couldn't breathe.

A quiet older man smashed the tips of my markers as he inked black spots across the face on the paper in front of him, mirroring his emotionless face that couldn't express the overwhelming, paralyzing pain inside.

A trauma survivor sketched yellow lightning bolts shooting up and down his spine, counterbalanced by gray weights of shame crushing his shoulders. His drawings helped him name what would keep him from moving through life and relationships in the way he wanted. Until then he'd felt stuck because of what he was holding inside.

A Sacred Invitation

What's happening in our body is not irrelevant noise to tune out. When we read certain psalms, we can almost imagine the colors and shapes the psalmists would have drawn on their body outline worksheets. While tuning in so deeply with what stirs within may be new to us, we can see clearly that it isn't a modern adaptation in the Judeo-Christian faith.

I can imagine a voice reaching for a red marker to illustrate their heart becoming hot inside, like a fire burning.[10] I can picture a psalmist drawing an alert and anxious gaze to match their cry, "You hold my eyes open with hypervigilance."[11]

I can see another drawing spirals in the outline of their head, saying, "I'm swirling in my thoughts," before extending their drawing outside of the body, coloring in the fear and panic coursing through their whole body.[12]

I picture another voice using storm clouds to depict their words, talking about how they are going through life, gloomy and dark, losing strength, numb and crushed as the light of their eyes leaves them.[13] I imagine others sketching out the anxiety that makes them feel as if their body is knotted up, twisted and bent out of shape, with their heart fluttering as anxiety expands far and wide inside them like a wildfire.[14]

Alongside these panicked drawings, I envision a calm voice sketching out the melody sung by their settled heart that's embedded in joy and anchored in security.[15] I can see another using bright colors to paint the delight in their soul, as if they've just finished a sweetly filling meal.[16]

And in one of my favorite images, gentle brushstrokes would show the secure bliss of a soothed and tender soul, resting quietly, like a small child resting against her mother.[17]

These ancient voices, preserved as sacred Scripture, invite us to sing in harmony with them, tuning in to what's stirring within as we move through the messiness of life and faith. Through joy and sorrow, they show us that what is happening in our body intersects with what's happening in our relationship with God, all the way to the depths of our soul. Their words remind us that our faith tradition is not centered on our thinking brain alone, but instead engages the entirety of our embodied being.

When we listen to what our body has to tell us, we can join these ancient voices and tap into what's happening beneath the surface. As we slow down and listen in, we can start to connect with the facets inside that have often been forgotten or neglected, and need our care.

PAUSE & PLAY:

WHAT'S HAPPENING INSIDE?

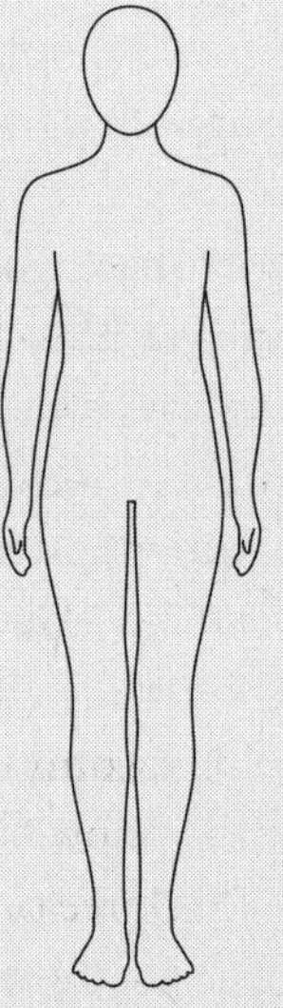

On a blank piece of paper, draw a simple outline of a body like the example shown. If that feels stressful, search "body outline template" online to find an image you can print or trace. Gather colored pencils, markers, or different-colored pens and highlighters. Moving through the list of emotions below, use shapes, images, and color to depict how you experience them in your body:

Sadness
Happiness
Fear
Anger
Disgust
Excitement

Ask yourself the following questions as you consider how you experience each emotion in your body:

Where in my body do I feel this emotion?

What does this emotion feel like in my body?

If this emotion could speak, what would it say?

CHAPTER 4

slowing down to listen in

Shortly after the loss of our beloved first cat, my husband and I began discussing whether we were ready to bring a new little bundle of fur home. One Thursday afternoon, I happened to check my phone at just the right moment, shortly after a pet rescue placed a request for someone to foster a mama cat and her five-week-old babies. I immediately replied, "I can leave right now and be there in twenty minutes!" What I failed to ask was, "How many of these five-week-old babies are there?"

Without explicitly naming how many kittens I had just committed to taking in, I'll just say that the shelter named the mom cat Snow White and each kitten after one of Snow White's seven friends. Feel free to take a moment to do the math.

When I arrived to pick them up, these little fur balls were in a large crate with their mom, an adorable conglomerate of black-and-white fur. We initially placed this fluffy family in a back office, setting up the room with their food and toys. During the day, we would close off the other doors in the house and let them venture down the hallway to the living room. They would often caravan together, scurrying with the precious pitter-patter of their paws.

One day, I opened the door to the office as usual to guide them down the hall to the living room. After making sure the doors to the other rooms were closed, I traveled with the pack to their favorite living room window. Once there, I heard what sounded like a faint and panicked meow. I did a quick head count—someone was missing.

I rushed down the hallway to the office to find an empty room, no kitten in sight. And then I heard it again, the panicked meow. This time it sounded like it was coming from the living room—the room I'd just left. So I ran back down the hallway past closed doors, only to hear the panicked meow coming from the other direction again. At this point I felt like I was starting to go crazy—as though bringing eight cats home wasn't enough of a sign!

Where was this kitten?

Tuning In with What's Been Shut Out

As I searched for the source of the panicked cries, the other kittens were making lots of noise with their own meows and movement. I stopped, slowed myself down, and tried to tune in to where the isolated little cries were coming from. I focused my attention on the one specific cry, moving closer and closer to the relentless squeals.

I finally figured out that Bashful—who I assure you was not bashful in any way—had led the pack and decided it would be fun to run into the hall bathroom before I could close the door. I hadn't noticed her black fur, which perfectly matched the dark room she scurried into. Once I opened the door, I saw her one-pound body sitting in the pitch-black, windowless bathroom. She was tiny and alone, meowing at the top of her little feline lungs. I immediately scooped her up in one hand, held her close for a few moments, and then reunited her with her fur family. I kept my eye on her as she went about her day as usual, watching birds out the window, fighting over toy mice with Doc and Grumpy, and snuggling up with Dopey and Sleepy for naps. She no longer needed to meow or cry to get my attention. She had what she needed and felt safe and secure to run, play, and rest—to simply *be*.

When I think about Bashful's tiny body crying, scared and alone in that dark room, I can't help but think about the parts of us that might be crying inside, longing to be heard and held close, but are instead drowned out by the other noise in and around us.

In our busy lives, it's easy to miss what's happening inside. Sometimes we simply move so fast, or what's happening in or around us is so noisy, that we don't even realize we've become disconnected from parts of ourselves, facets that have been forgotten or neglected. Even if we become more aware of these depths, our always-moving and always-distracted society can make us feel as if it's too inconvenient or overwhelming to tune in with everything happening inside.

Maybe we feel a sadness or hear a cry inside, but we don't know what to do with it. And if it feels like one more "problem" on our plate, we might just try to cut it off or tune it out. Maybe when we sit down with a cup of tea to journal and read, wrapped in a cozy blanket, we feel overwhelming sadness bubble up to the surface that seems to "ruin" the time we'd set aside to relax. Maybe we're exhausted, but when we finally get to bed at night, we lie there awake, unable to silence a thought or emotion and wondering where the off switch is to tune everything out. In each of these spaces, it's easy to see the parts of us that are "making noise" as problems we want to get rid of.

We often learn these postures from the people in our lives. If we grew up with parents or teachers criticizing us for the way we spoke, acted, or performed in school or sports, we're likely to criticize ourselves—especially those parts of ourselves that don't perform well or seem to get in the way of accomplishments. If we were told not to be a crybaby or to man up, we'll likely say similar things to the parts of us that well up with tears or want to crumble in heartache. We tell them, "You're not welcome here" in the same way someone first made that clear to us. And if we've been cut off from a space—whether a relationship, team, group, or family—because we weren't excelling, we'll reasonably sideline a part of us that doesn't seem to measure up, trying to eliminate this part of us before it gets us excluded.

But even when we try to disconnect from what's happening inside, that part of us continues to stir, even if we're not sure what to do with what's simmering beneath the surface.

In a painful irony, when we see these parts of us as problems that ruin things and should be cut off, we overlook that these parts are actually scared, wounded, or weary—in need of tender care. It's often easier to see a tiny kitten, scared and alone, and feel empathy to hold her close than it is to move toward parts of our own selves with this same kind of kindness. When I was searching my home for a squealing kitten, I didn't view Bashful's meows as a problem but instead, as communication—signals that helped me find her and help her. What if we could extend that same understanding to our own internal parts?

If I'm honest, tuning in with parts of myself that I felt were complicating my life took some significant reorientation. I did *not* view these parts of me as adorable kittens. Instead, I viewed them as problems that I wanted to mute right alongside the chronic pain in my body. But getting to know the most tender depths of my soul, along with the self-protective parts of me that guarded these depths, helped me understand why I often felt like I was fighting against my own self.

When we can make sense of why certain parts of us react in seemingly problematic ways, we're often pointed toward spaces inside that are in need of care. Before we dive in to work with these depths, we're going to consider what has shaped the ways we approach these tender spaces within.

PAUSE & PLAY:

LISTENING IN

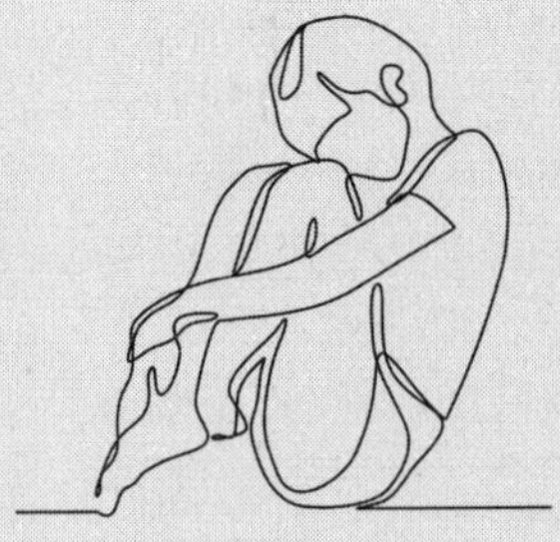

I'm curious if you can relate to hearing a cry from deep down in your soul, not knowing exactly who it is or how to get in touch with this part of you. If your mind were to sketch an image of what this feels like inside, what would that drawing look like? Before trying to figure out exactly how to do this exercise the "right way," see what it's like to simply notice what you naturally envision.

SLOWING DOWN TO LISTEN IN

As your mind imagines a part of you that resonates with being in a dark room, crying and alone, see what stirs inside as you read through the following:

How do you view this part of you? What emotions do you feel?

How do you imagine the posture and facial expression of this part?

What do you notice happening in your body as you reflect on these questions?

Describe any compassion, or lack of compassion, you feel toward this part. In what ways, if any, does that make you want to move toward it and care for this part?

List anything, such as frustration and overwhelm, that makes you want to move away from this part.

Now, imagine another person in a dark room. Try to imagine a friend or family member you love dearly, someone you cherish and adore. Imagine this person is crying and all alone.

As you imagine this scene, how do you view this person?

How is this similar to or different from the posture you have toward a part of yourself?

All Parts Sacred

When I began slowing down, I heard cries in the depths of my soul that I didn't know what to do with. Years into this process, one of the ways I tried to find healing for these spaces was by meeting with a pastor, knowing the pain I was carrying had pierced my soul.

I walked into his office feeling tension inside. I didn't want to entirely expose what felt like a mess in my internal world, but at the same time, I was exhausted from trying to wrestle through on my own. I sat down in a beige chair, situating a pillow behind me for back support and crossing my legs in a self-protective posture. I began to peel back layers of a dark night of the soul, letting parts of me have a voice that seemed to be complicating my life. These parts of me couldn't stop roaring, wondering, *Where is God?* and *Why does it seem as though God doesn't care, like at all?* In harmony with cries we see in the Psalms, I let the depths of my soul speak with honesty, saying, "I don't see God anywhere, and I don't see any hope."

As I was mid-sentence, the pastor interrupted me. "Okay, let's stop right there," he said. "It sounds like you're getting caught up in all this. I'm going to say a prayer, and you'll repeat after me, one line at a time. Ready?"

Outwardly, I said, "Yes, of course," taken off guard and not wanting to refuse to pray. Inwardly, I felt like time froze, unable to make sense of his response. I sat there repeating statements like, "God, I am so sorry I have not had the faith in You that You ask of us," and "Please help me be more obedient to You."

The prayers the pastor asked me to repeat didn't reference God's love or care as a refuge in grief or distress. His words didn't reflect or point me to God's compassion, grace, loyal love, or faithful kindness. I felt like a puppy who had just been shamed, told to put my tail between my legs before God. There was no room held to venture into the intersections of God's mercy and our pain. It felt like I had just gone to a physician for a gaping wound, but rather than tending to the injury with care, the physician had inflicted even more damage. I left deeply aware that my pain did not seem to matter to this pastor, and he made it seem as though this pain also did not matter to God.

Embedded Beliefs

When I left that pastor's office, I knew something wasn't right. My words had echoed ancient cries of the psalmists' songs, "Why do you hide your face?" and "Why do you stand far away?"[1] I couldn't help but wonder, *Why was it a problem to speak these honest words today, sentiments that have been preserved as sacred Scripture?*

As I tried to make sense of the meeting, I reflected on the assumptions that had shaped our conversation. From my training in interpreting ancient texts and my work as a therapist, I was aware that we all bring assumptions to different kinds of interactions—like embedded beliefs that we carry with us, even if they're never spoken out loud.[2] And even if these aren't explicitly stated, it doesn't mean that they aren't communicated at a gut level or known in our body.

So, I started to get curious about these beneath-the-surface beliefs that were present with us in that room. It became clear there were assumptions made about the depths I was speaking from—that these depths were disobedient, lacking in faith, stubborn, and bad. Along with this perspective, the solution presented was that I should silence what was stirring within and simply try to be more obedient. There was no compassion in this equation.

But in the famous line of Exodus 34:6—when God calls out to Moses, passing before him on Mount Sinai—wasn't *compassionate* the first word spoken to tell us who God is? And while it can be easy for words about God's compassion and grace to feel like platitudes we're desensitized to, I was also reminded of my Hebrew coursework that taught me the root noun of this Hebrew word for *compassionate* is the word *womb*—painting a picture of a mother who responds to her infant's cries with tender care.[3] Rather than being a random word that is only found once in an obscure passage, God's compassion reverberates throughout Scripture with the words from Exodus 34:6 being the most referenced passage within the Hebrew Bible.

And wasn't the embodiment of God's love and mercy in the person of Christ stirred with compassion when witnessing human pain and suffering? And before you might think that I'm overdramatizing the language here, let me share with you about my favorite Greek word in the New Testament. When we read in the Gospels that Christ was moved with compassion,[4] the Greek verb used—*splanchnizomai*—literally means to be so moved that you viscerally feel it in the depths of your being, deep down in your internal organs. The picture painted for us of Immanuel, God with us, is one of deeply embodied compassion.

I couldn't help but wonder, *Why then does our view of God and God's posture toward us so frequently miss this mark?* Reflecting beyond the one interaction I had with that pastor, I started to consider just how much we can internalize assumptions that we receive from others, projecting them onto our own selves. Whether we've received shaming messages from a faith community, a family, or anywhere else, the damage runs deep.

Just as the pastor had made assumptions about my heart and faith, we can embody beliefs that cause us to engage reactively with hurting parts of ourselves, shaming them rather than caring for them. Sadly, beliefs like these will often also shape how we assume God engages with these parts of us—distorting our view of a deeply compassionate God, causing us to instead imagine a God who shames us.

So, before we start to tune in more deeply with our internal world, let's first explore assumptions we might be bringing with us that could distort our view of things. As you read through the list below, I invite you to be curious about what rings true and whether you would add other embedded beliefs to make this list feel complete:

Embedded belief: Every part of us should automatically and consistently know and trust that God is good and reflect that in our thoughts, feelings, and behavior.

Embedded belief: We are being stubborn or controlling if any part of us is (seemingly) "refusing" to trust God, whether that be in thought, feeling, or behavior. Any sign of perceived resistance in our souls should be condemned as sin.

Embedded belief: The parts of us that appear resistant and stubborn just want control or reveal a lack of faith and are therefore sinful and bad.

Embedded belief: We need to somehow get rid of these parts of us that are bad in order to grow spiritually. Once we change our thoughts to align with correct theology, our behaviors will rightly align with correct theology. Any feelings that are not in line with accurate theology need to be dismissed and disposed of.

For some people, the list above may feel harsh and overstated. For others, these words may feel understated—not strong enough to match their experiences. Wherever you are, I invite you to consider the assumptions and stories that have shaped how you interact with what happens inside of you—your emotions, thoughts, and body sensations, all wrapped up in your embodied being that includes your heart, mind, body, soul, and more.

When we take the time to clearly spell out embedded beliefs like this, we can see that they are fundamental misunderstandings of how God wired our embodied being, reducing us too narrowly to thought and behavior. They don't account for the mysterious complexities of how we know and experience life beyond our thinking brain, down to our gut-level knowing and feeling.

Without taking the time to explore these kinds of assumptions, we run the risk of trying to force parts of ourselves into behavior modification, missing opportunities to offer them dignity and understanding—let alone to invite them into God's unending tender care.

The list below offers compassionate perspectives in contrast with the embedded beliefs above. These offer a more holistic view of how we are created, along with room for God's patient love and grace. Move through the list slowly, noticing how these statements resonate differently from the ones above:

Compassionate perspective: Every facet of us may not know or feel connected to God in the same way, whether this is expressed in our thinking brain, experienced nonverbally at a gut level, or understood in some other way in our body.

Compassionate perspective: Some depths of our soul might need to get acquainted with God in a new way, building trust in different ways than other parts of ourselves have. This might include accessing parts of us that are connected to our gut-level knowing and our body's perception of safety, beneath our thinking brains.

Compassionate perspective: All facets of us are woven in our embodied being, bearing God's image, which was declared good.[5] All parts of us are therefore first and foremost sacred. Experiences of pain shape wounds and fear in various parts of us.

Compassionate perspective: The overarching narrative of God's restorative work is about making all things new and right. Parts of us that are scared and hurting most need a compassionate response like the one lived out in Christ's ministry—an embodiment of God's mercy and lovingkindness. Encountering God's mercy and grace cultivates holistic and restorative formation, rather than fragmenting seemingly "good" parts of us from shamed "bad" parts of us.

I want to pause here and say that reorienting embedded beliefs might feel hopeful, threatening, or a confusing combination of the two. Our body often has a visceral response when we start to detangle assumptions we hold beneath the surface, and rightfully so. When something feels known, we might feel inclined to trust it above new ideas, even those that more accurately reflect what's true.

It might take time to work through the differences in these lists, and you might find it meaningful to create your own. Take the time you need. In future chapters, if you notice that your posture toward your internal world includes frustration, criticism, or shame, I invite you to come back to these lists to explore if any of these embedded beliefs seem to be informing those reactions.

As we turn the page and begin a new section, we'll continue to slow down, tuning in with what's happening inside our body. We'll explore what moves inside us, and how this moves us through life, all beneath our conscious awareness. And as we connect with what's going on beneath the surface, we can start to work with those movements, rather than feeling like they're working against us. Before we carry on, let's slow down with the prompts below.

PAUSE & PLAY:

SITTING WITH COMPASSION

Looking back to the list of embedded beliefs on page 56, take time to slow down and notice what reactions they elicit in your body. Whether it's anxiety, overwhelm, numbness, or anything else, simply observe how this feels in your body. Be gentle with yourself, giving yourself time and space to explore what's stirring inside.

See what it's like to settle in where you are, not ignoring the feelings, but letting yourself know you are anchored in this moment. If it feels helpful, consider slowly getting in touch with each of your five senses as you continue taking some deep breaths. Rather than trying to breathe your feelings away, see what it's like to breathe with them.

Next, see if it might feel different to consider these embedded beliefs if they were held by another person, someone you love deeply, or if you'd like, an adorable crying kitten. As you do this, notice how your assumptions and posture toward another being are different from how you approach yourself.

The second list of perspectives we looked at (see pages 57–58) points us to God's compassion, which we sometimes feel disconnected from or receive confusing messages about. How does it sit with you to imagine how moved Christ must have been to feel compassion deep down in the depths of internal organs—to imagine God with us, feeling with us? If any parts of you aren't ready to think about or feel this, see what it's like to be gentle with yourself, not forcing yourself into behavior modification or trying to muster up a spiritually shiny Sunday school answer. If you'd like to reflect on this more, I invite you to move through the questions below:

> *In what ways does the mention of Christ's compassion bring relief or comfort?*
>
> *In what ways does the mention of Christ's compassion make you uncomfortable?*
>
> *In what ways does the mention of Christ's compassion stir up any fear or grief inside you?*

PART TWO

tune in with the body

CHAPTER 5

tuning in with internal movements

Our eyes locked, growing wide as we spoke to each other only through the intensity of our stare. We knew we were thinking the same exact thing: *We're in for a bumpy ride!* We fastened our seatbelts as quickly as we could, bracing ourselves for the journey ahead of us. And while you might think we were about to take off on a roller coaster, the two of us were simply hopping in the car for a mundane drive down the road with a beloved friend in the driver's seat, a friend whose driving we knew all too well.

During my college years, this was a regular occurrence, all depending on who was driving the car. As dear friends who moved alongside each other through our days and car rides, we got to know the cadences of each other's movements well enough to anticipate what we were in for. Each of our driving styles had a different kind of rhythm as we approached and left each traffic light, leaving us either calm while enjoying the ride, or bracing ourselves to avoid feeling like we were about to slam our heads against the seat in front of us.

While I liked to think I was one of the better drivers back then, years later I realized that I felt that way because I was so used to the abruptness of my own movements. When I was behind the wheel, I would cruise ahead, stopping suddenly and only when necessary to obey red lights and stop signs. And while I'd still like to believe I wasn't the *worst* driver of the group (you know who you are and you know that I love you!), I now cringe when I imagine what it was like to ride in the back seat when I drove. I never thought twice about rushing and whipping the vehicle around, or wondered what that was like for the other passengers. I was just on autopilot.

Outside the car, I charged through life in the same way—at full speed. I never noticed the ways I would speed up or slow down, shifting gears internally, or the ways that different parts of me were involved in these different movements. This is where we're going next: exploring how we move through life in ways that feel so normal to us that we rarely notice our driving style, or who's behind the wheel.

In part 1, we began slowing down to explore what's happening inside us, beneath our thinking brain. As we continue our journey, we'll tune in with the core muscle memory that moves our embodied being through life, along with the *parts* of us that play different roles in those movements. We'll approach this with curiosity to cultivate a restorative awareness of where we feel most disconnected or stuck, the spaces where we might most need tender care. With curiosity and care as our foundation, we'll be well positioned to tend to our internal worlds, exploring new movements as we work *with*, instead of *against*, ourselves.

Traffic Signals

When we are driving to a place we've never been before or preparing to merge onto a busy highway, we might pause to consider our best course of action, consulting our thinking brain as our feet and hands move us where we want to go. Most of the time though, we drive our cars without a lot of conscious thought. We know to speed up or slow down by paying attention to traffic signals. Our foot will press on the gas when we see a green light—we don't even have to think about it. Similarly, our foot will automatically press the brakes to stop when we see a red light. If an animal or car surprises us, nearly causing an accident, we will slam on the brakes or swerve with our foot still on the gas. We do this before our thinking brain has time to analyze all the details.

Something similar happens in our everyday lives, determining whether our body will press on an internal *gas pedal* or an *internal brake system.*[1] When things happening around us cue our body to stop or go, we instinctively slow down or speed up. If everything around us (and inside us!) seems fine, we calmly coast ahead or rest idly as we move through our day.

The traffic signals that tell our bodies to speed up or slow down can be any sort of cue, big or small. We might look at the time and realize we're late—cue immediate adrenaline to hurry up! Or maybe we look at the time and realize we have time to spare—cue a sigh of relief. Or maybe we receive a text message that stops us dead in our tracks—cue our gut dropping and our breath stopping for a moment. None of these cues come with explicit instructions telling us to speed up or slow down. Instead, our body navigates internal and external cues all around us, all the time, all beneath the awareness of our thinking brain.

Researcher Stephen Porges calls this process *neuroception* (*neuro* for brain + per*ception*).[2] We can think of this as a 24-7 subconscious scanner that's trying to determine our level of safety at any given moment. If our neuroception detects any threat in our present circumstances, our body will be prompted within milliseconds to try to move away from or through that threat. Our body is innately wired to return us to a sense of safety, either by pressing on a sort of internal gas pedal or by utilizing an internal brake system.

When we press on the gas, we speed up to move through distress or stressors that might be in front of us. When our brakes engage, our body and mind slow down. When our brakes release, we're able to access some energy and movement, similar to what happens when we release the brakes on a bicycle.[3] Our life is like one continual conversation between our neuroception and the gas pedal and brake system that are wired inside us, with our body instinctively speeding up or slowing down in an attempt to safely move us through our days.

These subconscious processes keep our heart rate and breathing regulated. Without them, our heart could beat faster or slower than would be safe or sustainable. In a perfect world where our baseline experience of life is one of perpetual safety, calm, and rest, we would need this brake system only to gently slow us down into deeper rest or, when released, to gently give us some energy to play and enjoy exciting experiences.

It's pleasant to experience our brake system slowing us down when we're sinking into a warm nap on a beach vacation. But life is not one long beach vacation. We live in a world with unending stressors. Often when we are stressed, our body fuels us with adrenaline, mobilizing us to charge ahead. If we're pushed to a limit beyond what we can sustainably navigate, we'll slow down and come to a stop, not pleasantly but in a jarring, burned-out kind of way. If our body becomes overwhelmed, our brake system can slam us to a halt. In this kind of deceleration, our body starts to fold, overriding the gas pedal and bringing us to a disorienting stop.

These innate movements are often a good thing, especially when it comes to our physical safety. Think about how your hand automatically pulls back from a hot stovetop or you instinctively slow down when you think you might see a rattlesnake on the trail ahead. In these scenarios, it's easy to be grateful for the way we are designed, since we can clearly see how it helps us move through life safely. In many scenarios, however, the body logic that informs our movements doesn't feel so clear or linear, especially situations in which emotional and relational factors are in play—so basically, all of life!

In the same way that our body sets off alarm bells when our hand is on a hot stovetop or when we see a rattlesnake that could harm or kill us, alarms sound when we perceive emotional or relational threats. In relationships, we might experience this as our emotions getting heightened in conflict, with our thoughts and reactions speeding up. At other times we might feel the brake system slam us into shutdown, immobilizing us from engaging with the person in front of us. When this happens, our body decides for us that the distress in front of us is simply too much. This is what was happening when I collapsed on the bathroom floor after months of not sleeping in a season of unsustainably high stress.

The conversation between our neuroception and these movements happens subconsciously in the deepest parts of our brain and body, all beneath rational thought. This is why it can sometimes feel like we are being driven through life rather than sitting in the driver's seat. If we're in the car with a friend who is driving much faster or slower than we would prefer, we might get slightly irritated. It's a completely different kind of frustration when we notice our body moving in a way that seems to be working against us or our longings.

Depending on how the muscle memory of your internal gas pedal and brake system has been shaped, it might feel like you're in a car that's a little too quick to go with the gas, a car that's nearly impossible to get to a full stop, or a car that's difficult to get going or to slow down. Or maybe you find yourself feeling confused because your body seems to press the gas pedal and the brakes at the same time, seemingly stalling out. Or maybe the biggest issue is that your movements seem to be working against you, and putting mind over matter isn't getting you where you want to go.

If slowing down doesn't feel emotionally safe to our internal system, our body, beneath the awareness of our thinking brain, will decide to either press on the gas pedal or pump the brakes. In order to work *with* our body and move through life differently, we need to understand which parts of us have shaped this internal muscle memory.

PAUSE & PLAY:

CONNECTING WITH CUES

It may feel strange to think about our body making decisions beneath the awareness of our thinking brain, speeding us up or slowing us down. As we tune in with what's happening inside, let's play with a story so we can better recognize the decisions being made beneath the surface. Read through the narrative below, being curious to notice when the main character may be shifting gears internally, beneath her conscious awareness. Pay attention to the times she seems to be shifting into one of these speeds listed below:

- gently or firmly pressing the gas pedal
- cautiously reaching for the brakes
- slamming on the brakes
- easing on the brakes, gently cruising ahead
- parked and stationary, not moving

Alex wakes to the sound of birds chirping, and she notices a gentle sunbeam dancing as it streams through her bedroom window. She takes a deep breath, satisfied after a restful night of sleep. Her whole body feels as if it has melted into her cozy bed, and she savors the sense of actually feeling rested. Then she looks at the clock. As soon as she sees the time, she realizes she is late.

Without a moment to wonder how or why her alarm didn't go off, she rushes out of bed. She knows she'll barely make it to work on time, even if she moves as quickly as she can. She needs to be at an 8 a.m. meeting, and it's already 7:33 a.m. She snatches the first work-appropriate outfit she can throw on while simultaneously letting the dog out, barking at him to make it quick!

As she flies down the street in her car, Alex starts to breathe a sigh of relief. Maybe, just maybe, she'll make it to work right on time. Before she can fully exhale, though, she turns the corner to find a long string of stopped traffic in front of her, completely blocking access to any other route she might take. She brings her car to a full stop, fuming inside as she sits there helplessly, completely stuck. Her thoughts race a mile a minute, spinning in harmony with her heartbeat. The longer her car stays put, the higher her blood pressure seems to go. Soon she feels like she is going to burst.

Finally the standstill clears, and Alex slowly continues on her way. She arrives to work later than she ever has before. She feels embarrassed and defeated. Despite cringing inside, she knows she has to go to the meeting she is late to. She feels dread with each step she takes across the conference room to her seat. All eyes are on her, and she can barely breathe.

The meeting eventually wraps up. A colleague who needs her expertise to address an issue stops her on the way out, distracting her from her embarrassment. She carries on with her day, eventually forgetting that she had been late. And before she knows it, it's time to get back in the car and head home. She survived, and everything ended up being okay. Her worst fears of upsetting her boss never materialized.

Alex had planned to meet with a friend that night, but right after work, the friend texts to cancel. She realizes she has just gained over two hours for the evening, time that hasn't been allotted to anything yet. She thinks through the several errands she needs to run, mentally stacking up a to-do list for the evening. After she finishes those, she stops at one of her favorite parks for a short walk, something she rarely has time for.

As she starts to move, her body mimics the speed and intensity that normally carries her through busy days, but she doesn't even notice. Her mind swirls through a presentation she has to give the next day and the food she needs to prepare for a family gathering that weekend. She charges ahead on the path, not noticing new blooms to her right or the start of a sunset to her left.

Across the field from her, she spots a dog with a golden coat playing fetch with his owner. The dog is clearly living his best life, sprinting with glee as he hunts down a favorite toy and brings it back to his trusted human. The joy and freedom of this dog's play interrupts her train of thought, knocking the wind out of the momentum that was fueling her.

She watches the dog bounce with each step, and that inspires a different kind of spring in her own stride. Rather than rushing ahead on the path, her body starts to move in a different rhythm, not driven by pressure but instead gently yielding to the present moment.

The dog cannot contain his excitement, evident in his ecstatic wiggles, and Alex smiles, laughing under her breath. Then she takes the deepest inhale she has all week. For a few moments she forgets what time it is, what day it is, and the many tasks on her to-do list. She is simply there, delighting in the scene playing out in front of her, cruising along as she continues on the path.

Consider the list provided above the narrative, curiously noticing where you think Alex was shifting gears between each kind of movement. Rather than trying to get the "right" answers, simply notice what happens inside of you as you map out her pace throughout the story.

Who's Driving the Car

If we are convinced that our thinking brain is in the driver's seat and moving us through life, we're likely to feel frustrated and confused about why we keep driving in circles or down roads that don't lead us where we want to go. When we start to tap into all the facets that make up the whole of us, we can begin to get a sense of which part is in the driver's seat and what causes that part to shift gears in a specific rhythm. Like the characters of the *Inside Out* movies, different strands of us make up the whole, forming one multifaceted perspective of how we see the world. And just as in these movies, when one character inside takes over and operates the control board from their specific perspective, we tend to move through life more reactively.

If a socially anxious part of me is thrown into a situation where I don't know anyone, I might feel panicked, trying to figure out how to get rid of the pressure I feel inside. I don't calmly consider that I'll be okay if I stand alone in a room full of people who all know each other or that it might just take some time to enter a conversation. If this perspective takes over, I'm likely to either try to leave the room or figure out my quickest way into a conversation. Both of these options are fueled by stress and discomfort. I'll move into one of these outcomes if I stay in my panicked perspective, not consulting the perspective of more patient and long-term thinking parts of me.

When one part of us takes over, we lose the fuller perspective of all parts of us that make up the whole of our embodied being. This is why it can be helpful to imagine different parts of us as different drivers who hop in the driver's seat and start driving in different ways—some quick to press on the gas pedal and others more likely to hit the brakes, some speedy to get out of discomfort and others slow moving to act.

In my own life, when my neuroception senses everything is fine, my perspective is calm and parts of me can either slow down in concert with the brake system, or fill me with energy as my body gently releases the brakes. After I've taken a getaway to the mountains with my husband or spent a cozy week filled with snuggles from my nieces and nephews,

I'm often cushioned by the connection I shared in these spaces, which calms my entire body and anchors my perspective in a sense of safety. From this calm place, I don't see danger or threats on the road ahead and can flexibly carry on with my day.

But when my neuroception is activated by a sight or sound that seems like potential danger, a hypervigilant part of me shoves her way into the driver's seat, reactively pressing her foot on the gas. This is the muscle memory she knows: She wants to be ready for anything that might come my way, ready to jump into action at any moment. Her driving is fueled by fear, and she is scanning everything around me, assuming there is danger to look out for and steer clear of. She is a woman on a mission, moving fast, refusing to slow down or stop until she is convinced my surroundings are safe. If I'm walking alone at night and sense someone might be following me or if I feel a snake biting my ankle (yes, true story!), my body will be anything but calm and my perspective will be vigilant, scanning my surroundings for additional threats. And in these scenarios, I'm grateful for that.

When I'm exhausted, barely holding on and pushed to the point of overwhelm, my body comes to a screeching halt. The brakes override everything else, stopping the whole car—stopping all of me. From this perspective, I'm not interested in pressing forward or carrying on. I'm solely concerned with slowing down and stopping, not so much out of a thoroughly formulated plan but out of a reactive instinct. My body senses that if I don't stop or pull over, I'm not going to make it. Whatever I'm trying to drive through is too much, like I'm caught in a fierce storm with rain coming down harder than I can manage, keeping me from seeing the road ahead. The muscle memory of this place says, *This is too much. I need to stop.* And here I brake with rigidity rather than ease, just as I did the day my body collapsed on the bathroom floor.

When using this driving analogy in therapy, one of my favorite things to do is open space for all parts of my clients to have a voice and be heard. Within this analogy, the car is like our embodied being that includes all facets of us as we move through life. After hearing about internal conflict or an overwhelming emotion, my prompt to them is simply, "In this scenario, which part of you is in the driver's seat? What are they thinking, feeling, saying? Where do you imagine other parts of you in the car, and what are they thinking, feeling, or saying?"

My clients tell me about the parts of them that say, *Let's go!* when something pokes an old wound. Suddenly, they feel fiercely defensive and protective, ready for a fight. Others tell me about the parts of them that simply say *Nope!* when way too much is asked of them. When the unseen depths of them can't take it any longer, they pull the car over to a full stop. My favorite driving metaphors include heated conversations between the driver and other parts in the back seat. Reminiscent of family car rides, there's often a driver shouting like a stressed-out parent: *Everyone stop fighting or I will turn this car around right now!*

I've also witnessed quieter parts of my clients that are tucked away in the car. They sit silently in the back, longing for a smoother ride, or wishing they could leap out of the car to escape the discomfort or anxiety they know they're driving into. I can feel the pain of the parts that have been silenced, shoved in the trunk of the car, tolerated in the most minimal of ways, feeling unwanted and abandoned—or even the parts of them that have been kicked out of the car, left along the side of the road years ago. Each part holds a story we can tune in with and hold with compassionate and tender care.

Just as we can feel we're at the mercy of another person's driving when we're a passenger in a car, we sometimes feel this way moving through our daily life. Until we get in tune with the way our body automatically steps on the gas or applies the brakes, we might wonder why we react as we do, shaming ourselves or viewing ourselves as our own worst enemy. Noticing the movements directed by our gas pedal and brake system can help us make sense of the different parts of us that both shape and have been shaped by the muscle memory our body holds, the muscle memory that moves us through life.

We can better understand why we move through life in the ways we do when we see that our thinking brain is not the only driver in the car. And when we start to connect with more of the strands that are woven together in the whole of us, we can work *with* them rather than feel as if there's an uncontrollable battle over who gets to control the wheel and pedals. As we work *with* rather than *against* the facets inside us, we can move toward smoother rides that take us where we most long to go.

PAUSE & PLAY:

STOP AND GO

As you think about an internal gas pedal and brake system, what happens inside your body? Consider which parts of you seem to be associated with each of the following, and how you experience these parts of you taking the driver's seat in your body. Fill in the blanks of the following statements:

Examples:

When it feels like a gas pedal inside is pressed with excitement and joy, it feels like ***electricity/sunshine/warmth/anticipation*** *in my body, and the part of me that's in the driver's seat is* ***a younger version of me who feels more free****.*

When it feels like a gas pedal inside is pressed on in stress or panic, it feels like ***lightning bolts/shouting/fire/pressure*** *in my body, and the part of me that's in the driver's seat is* ***a rigid/anxious version of me who is worried and not thinking clearly****.*

When it feels like a gas pedal inside is pressed with excitement and joy, it feels like ____________________ in my body, and the part of me that's in the driver's seat is ________________ ____.

When it feels like a gas pedal inside is pressed on in stress or panic, it feels like ____________________ in my body, and the part of me that's in the driver's seat is ________________ ____.

When it feels like the brakes inside me are engaged so I am free to rest and savor what's in front of me, it feels like ____________________ in my body, and the part of me that's in the driver's seat is ____________________________________

____.

When it feels like the brakes inside me are pressed in overwhelm, shutting my system down, it feels like ______________________ *in my body, and the part of me that's in the driver's seat is*

____.

When it feels like the gas pedal and brake inside are activated at the same time, it feels like ________________________________ *in my body, and the parts of me that are in conflict as they try to navigate the car are* ____________________________________.

CHAPTER 6

tuning in with internal states

I wanted to scream—but I couldn't make a sound. Only a few feet from me stood hundreds of pounds of an authentic Smoky Mountain black bear.

Moments earlier, I'd been blissfully hiking a narrow trail with my sister-in-law Sarah. We had the path to ourselves, soaking in the leaves and trees that wrapped around us. To the right was a steep forested incline. To the left was a plunging wooded drop-off.

That morning I had just met a large deadline, and I'd planned this hike to help me exhale and settle after weeks of intensive work. Until this moment, I'd felt stress leave my body and relief sink in with every step. The birds, trees, and mountains anchored around us were a sweet escape from my computer screen. Then we turned a sharp corner, only to come face-to-face with an enormous bear.

Now, let me just say that not only was this the largest bear we had ever seen, but it was also the most beautiful bear we had ever seen. He looked like a massive teddy bear that had just been washed and blow-dried at the salon, his perfectly manicured and groomed coat shining as sun streamed in through the trees and bounced off his head.

For a split second, I was tempted to stand in awe like the tourists who take pictures of bears that scurry in front of them, unaware that these adorable creatures have put their lives in danger. That split second did not last long. Apart from my thinking brain, which hadn't yet fully acknowledged what was happening, my body became tense, aware that I was feet away from a creature that could seriously harm us. There was no one else around—just us, the narrow trail, the steep forested incline to the right, the plunging wooded drop-off to the left, and that massive and beautiful bear just in front of us.

Sarah and I grabbed each other's arms and started to cautiously walk backward, hoping to get back around the bend we'd just come from. We kept our eyes on the bear and the drop-off, and I racked my brain for what to do when encountering this kind of bear. My thinking brain could remember certain rules applied for specific kinds of bears. I knew that I knew the different bear rules, but I couldn't remember what they were right then.

I quietly whispered to Sarah, "What do we do with this kind of bear?"

She confidently and quietly replied, "We need to get as big and loud as we can."

My insides geared up. After we'd cautiously backed ourselves around the bend, the bear was no longer in sight. We knew, though, that he was still near. I wasn't sure if this felt better or worse. Regardless, I knew it was now time to get big and loud in hopes of spooking the bear so he'd scurry into the woods.

We picked up large rocks and threw them on the ground, and we banged sticks. Then Sarah started yelling at a decibel I'd never heard before.

I stood beside her, knowing I should be yelling with her but unable to make a noise. She was pulling *all* of the weight in the getting loud department. Now, I've never been described as a quiet person. I'm often loud and have no problem being loud. You'd think this would translate well into this moment, right? Somehow, it didn't.

In paralyzing terror, my body pressed down with full force on both the gas pedal and brake system. I wanted to shout, but I could not make a sound.

Autonomic Landscape

When our body presses on the gas, the brakes, or both, the parts of us that make up the whole of us are moving in tandem with what's happening in our *autonomic nervous system*. We can think of our autonomic nervous system as a core facet of our embodied being that regulates certain functions happening beneath our thinking brain—things like heart rate, blood pressure, breathing, and digestion. These functions keep us alive and breathing while we sleep. They're also what will pump us with adrenaline when we see a snake or a big, beautiful bear. Our autonomic nervous system automatically shifts gears depending on the cues our neuroception picks up, whether it's detecting cues of perceived safety or cues of perceived threat. Our autonomic nervous system then speeds us up or slows us down, either pressing on our internal gas pedal or our internal brake system (or a combination of the two!).

One of my favorite ways to invite people to connect with what's happening inside of us is to map out where we are in the three main states regulated by our autonomic nervous system, which are depicted on the next page.[1]

When we slow down to look at this illustration and ask, *Where am I?*, we're attempting to tune in with our body and the part(s) of us that are in the driver's seat. We are looking for cues to determine which one of these three states we are in: (1) Are we anchored in *safety*? (2) Are we activated in *stress*? or (3) Are we overwhelmed into *shutdown*?[2] While we'll look at these as three distinct states to help us connect with them conceptually, it's important to note that our body moves through them with a lot more nuance. We spend much of our life in mixed states—an overlap of more than one of these three states, which we'll explore in the chapters ahead.

Life is constantly full of cues, whether it's emails, everyday stressors, relationships, or painful wounds, that constantly move our body into the territory of stress or that lead to overwhelm and shutdown. These cues inform our neuroception—our body's perception of whether or not we're safe—signaling to us that we are no longer in a state of safety and need to move differently to try to get back there. When Sarah and I encountered

AUTONOMIC STATES

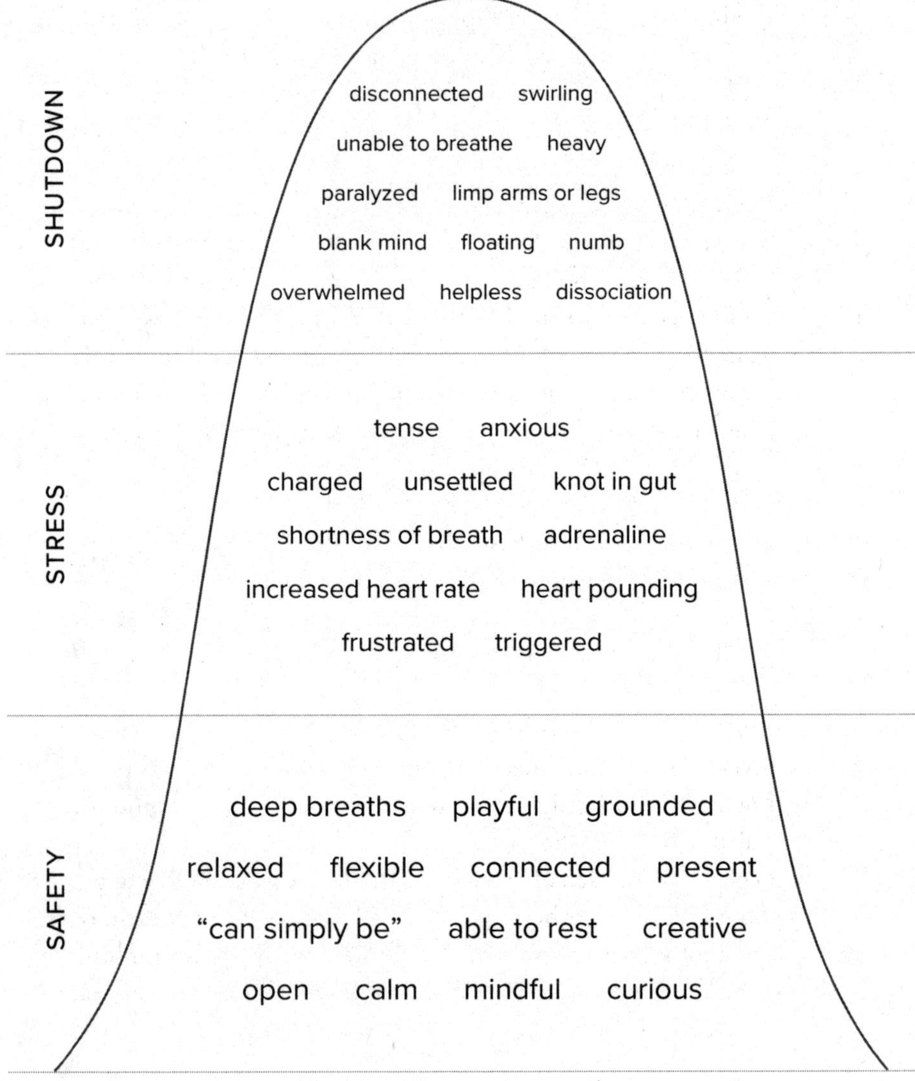

that beautiful bear, her neuroception cued a heavy foot on the gas pedal, driving her straight into a helpful state of stress that gave her energy to get big and loud. My neuroception, on the other hand, initially prompted a foot on the gas pedal but then another part quickly overrode this and slammed on the brakes. My body was entirely overwhelmed by what was in front of us—I was pushed so far into stress that I crossed over into shutdown.

As we learned in the last chapter, our body is wired with innate wisdom that discerns factors beneath the awareness of our thinking brain to help us survive. Remembering this is a game changer when we start to map out how different parts of us are intertwined with the muscle memory of our autonomic nervous system. Our reactions are not intended to complicate our life or cause problems—it's actually quite the opposite! These movements are instinctual and designed to keep us safe by helping us navigate distress and danger. So often parts of us that are tangled up in the reactions of our autonomic nervous system get scapegoated and shamed as though they're our enemies. In reality, these parts are our most loyal allies, riding the waves of our built-in wiring to move us through life.

As we tune in with our reactions, we can begin to understand how and why parts of us move through autonomic states as they do. Instead of viewing these reactions as problems to shame, we can work *with* these parts to learn new ways to move with and through our autonomic states. We can develop new muscle memory to press on our internal gas pedal or brakes, which is ultimately freeing both for those parts of us and for our embodied being as a whole.

As you get to know each of these states better, see what it's like to get curious about the way your body automatically moves through each, or from one to another, apart from any decision-making by your thinking brain. Let your body be curious to tune in with whichever parts of you come alive in each of these states.

State of stress

When we're in a state of stress, it's as if someone is turning up the volume inside. Our blood gets pumping, our breathing and heart rate increase, our thoughts often race, and our emotions are charged. When we're in this place, called the *sympathetic state*,[3] we feel like someone is stepping on that gas pedal inside us, fueling us to move.

This inner gas pedal is activated when our neuroception—our brain and body's perception of whether or not we're safe—perceives something in our environment that requires us to get activated, or mobilized into action, so that we can move through what's in front of us and return to a sense of safety.

If we come across a rattlesnake on a hike, we'll likely be glad that we are wired with this accelerator to fuel us with adrenaline, enabling us to run away from the snake. If the stress response is activated because we receive countless emails or text messages a day, we probably don't feel as grateful for it. When we chronically live in a state of stress, we often feel exhausted and stuck, and our body doesn't quite know how to gently press on the brakes to anchor us to a calm place or to gently release the brakes for a calm, regulated flow of energy.

State of shutdown

While we can think of our stress state as the gas pedal, we can think of the other two states as the brakes, though in two distinctly different ways. When our neuroception determines that a threat or stressor is more than we can feasibly move through, it cues our body to stop trying to move through the stressor with the gas pedal and instead use the brake system to shut things down in our body. It's our attempt at self-preservation.

No matter how hard our thinking brain might try to force us to keep going, certain circumstances push our body to the point where our neuroception will determine that the stress is too much, signaling the brakes to kick in. We become immobilized rather than mobilized, feeling frazzled or frozen, no longer fueled with adrenaline, but instead feeling depleted of any energy or hope. In this state, our thoughts, heart rate, breathing, and emotions are flattened.

Cues of overwhelm signal to our body that staying in a state of shutdown is the safest place to be until we can more securely find our way back to a felt sense of safety. Because the response to these cues happens beneath the conscious awareness of our thinking brain, we may feel disoriented in this space. We may notice that both the gas pedal and brakes are firing at the same time, freezing us in our tracks. In the face of a big beautiful bear, I could feel fear pumping through me while I simultaneously couldn't yell.

State of safety

When we enter a state of safety, our brake system works much differently than in shutdown. Instead of being coupled with overwhelm, the state of safety is coupled with connection, openness, and flexibility. When we're in this place, we have the most freedom to move through life. We are not being driven by reactive instincts trying to get us back to safety—we are already there! That enables our body to be at rest.

In this place, our neuroception senses that we have enough safety to take a deep breath, sink into a resting heart rate, and allow our thoughts and emotions to flow flexibly. We are the most grounded and able to connect with others, offering our presence and enjoying theirs. Rather than being distracted by possible risks or threats, we are anchored in the present in a way that facilitates creativity, curiosity, and play. If our body is anchored in a place of safety, we have the freedom and openness to release the brakes or gently work in tandem with our gas pedal in a way that stretches our system, instead of stressing it.[4]

Our body is remarkably designed to move flexibly between these three states, as well as combinations of them. However, if our starting point or anchored point is one of stress or shutdown, we will no longer be able to move flexibly between these states or combinations of them. Instead, our movements will be reactionary and rigid, driven by fear or stress.

Whether we want it to be true or not, many of us spend most of our life within a stress state, mistaking low-level stress for safety. When we live in stress, it's hard to know how to separate who we are from the version of us who shows up in the world in that state, the one who presses the gas pedal all the way down when taking the driver's seat. Like Alex from the last chapter, when this is our experience, our muscle memory, down to our autonomic nervous system, is so used to stress that it's where we live. As a result, we often feel stuck, unable to easily or fully sink into safety.

PAUSE & PLAY:

IDENTIFYING STATES

As you reflect on the questions below, see what it's like to set aside criticisms or judgments. You might take a deep breath as you imagine asking criticisms or judgments to give you space to reflect on these prompts.

- Turn back to page 78. When you look at the visual of the three states and think about your body experiencing safety, stress, or shutdown, what happens inside?
- Next, consider the body outline from chapter 3. Where would different emotions and body experiences fit into these three states? Are there ways that you resonate with a mixed state, overlapping between more than one of the three states? This might be excitement that is both anchored in safety and charged with energy, or feeling frozen as your body shuts down but is still charged with adrenaline.
- After considering this for yourself, what comes to mind when you think about a loved one or a pet experiencing safety, stress, or shutdown? For example, you might think about the embodied expressions of a person or furry friend who gets amped up in stress, flattened in overwhelm, or blissfully sinks into safety.
- If it's difficult to connect with these states, try to identify an animal or a cartoon character to represent each of these states. Consider: Who would they be and what would they look like? What would these caricatures do and say in each state? How would they move? What would their facial expressions be like? What would be the tones of their voices and the cadence of their words?

Before we continue on, if there are different words that best fit how you experience these three states (other than safety, stress, and shutdown), feel free to switch out these terms for what resonates most naturally for you.

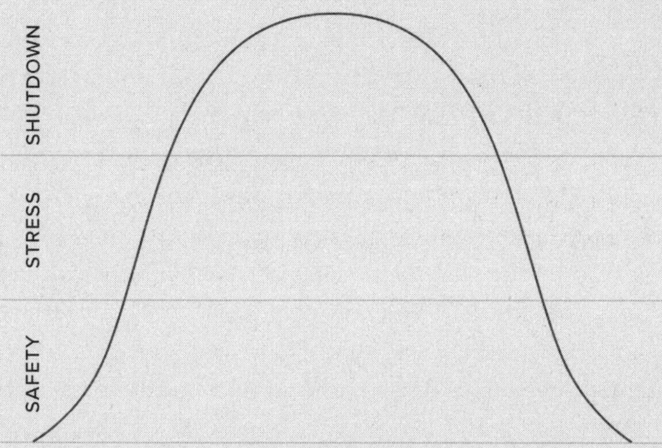

Body and Soul

I first saw a visual of these three autonomic states while in a doctor's office. Even though this was a place completely removed from spirituality, I felt as if I was looking at a map of the landscape of my soul, the terrain that parts of me would move through in tandem with my body. Something inside me immediately knew that these states were not entirely separate from the state of the soul—something I saw more and more clearly during meetings with my spiritual director.

I remember sitting down one day on the leather couch in Shari's office, placing a blanket over my lap. I tucked my feet underneath me as I tightly clutched what I had brought with me in my hands. At our last appointment, she had asked me to bring her something that represented the state of my soul. Part of me would have loved to bring in something like a flourishing bonsai tree, reflecting on what the firm roots and lush green leaves might represent inside of me.

Instead, feeling both curious and anxious, I handed her a Bible. From the moment I lifted it from my lap, pieces of the cover fell off. This Bible had been with me for years, through some of the darkest nights I had walked through. As it was literally crumbling before us, I resonated with its current state. Shari's eyes grew wide.

Nearly every inch of the faux leather cover was missing. The binding was disintegrating, and pages were falling out. It did not make a pretty picture, and it was by no means the shiny spiritual answer that a bonsai tree would have been to the question, "What is the state of your soul?" I wasn't sure how else to communicate what was happening inside.

To Shari and those around me, I appeared chipper and joyful most of the time. And in one way, those things were true. At the same time, however, I was tired inside, wholeheartedly weary. Without realizing it, I had spent a long time believing that this weariness was not supposed to intersect with my spirituality—that I should be strong enough and have a sturdy enough faith to keep my spirituality from being hindered by my flesh.

This was easier to navigate at a younger age with more energy and resilience. But then, the more life I walked through—including trauma, loss, and disappointments—the harder this became. I was quick to criticize and shame myself for being unable to control my thoughts and behavior as I thought I should be able to do. I felt frustrated with myself when I wasn't able to rest in perfect peace. I wondered if I couldn't surrender my rushing thoughts and anxiety-filled body in quiet trust because my faith was weak or because something was wrong with me.

It wasn't until I understood the different states of our autonomic nervous system that I could make sense of why I felt like this tattered Bible, and that this was not a reflection of an inherent flaw or weak faith. Then, with a window into how we are holistically wired, I had more clarity on what was going on beneath the surface: My spirituality was not separate from what was happening in my body. The state of my autonomic nervous system was mysteriously intertwined with the state of my soul.

When my body was in a state of stress, the impacts were not limited to my heart rate and breathing. My thoughts, perspective, and stirrings of my soul were involved as well—all interwoven in and reverberating through my one embodied being. And this was also true when my body was in a state of safety and rest, or overwhelm and shutdown.

The ancient Israelites seemed to understand and express this inherent connection, even if they didn't use clinical language to describe it. As we saw in chapter 3, their language in many psalms describes what's happening in their body, all fused together in their cries and praises to God. These authors didn't make divisions between their somatic experiences and their spirituality. Instead, they expressed the complexities of how these strands are interwoven in their human experience.

The psalmists didn't limit their communication with God to when they felt safe and secure. Their cries of distress, terror, and overwhelm demonstrate a deeply holistic spirituality that covers the entire autonomic landscape—all three states that our body moves through along with mixtures of these states. And now, across thousands of years, we can join with their voices, tapping into a fuller connection with the entirety of our being in an embodied spirituality.

When we are activated into anxiety, prone to panic in stress, or fueled with adrenaline, we can resonate with the psalmists' cries from thousands of years ago. We can know we are not alone as we identify with descriptions of their thoughts swirling and their hearts beating violently, like a woman writhing in labor.[5]

When we feel overwhelmed, as if our souls are collapsing into a state of shutdown, hopeless and resigned, we can sing in harmony with their ancient cries. We can name what it feels like to be crushed and numb, without light in our eyes.[6]

When we breathe in a sense of secure rest and safety, anchored in a calm and grounded body, we might remember the stillness of quiet waters in Psalm 23. In moments when our hearts are settled, we might resonate with our soul feeling satisfied, like we've sweetly savored a rich meal.[7]

In each of these places, what happens in our body is not entirely separate from our spirituality. When we tap into the mysterious intersection of the state of our body and the state of our soul, we can join with ancient sisters and brothers who were already singing about this thousands of years ago.

And as we map out the places we find ourselves, we can explore the possibility that God welcomes us when we reach out from any somatic state, longing to tend to us regardless of where we are in our autonomic landscape. We can embrace the messiness of these states, exploring the relief we feel when we don't force ourselves to try getting it together to come up with the shiniest Sunday school answer.

Sacred Spaces

It's so important to pause here and say that it is incredibly common for parts of us to have a hard time trusting or resting in a state of safety, let alone trusting or resting in God as an anchor of safety. As you reflect on the intersections of autonomic states and the state of the soul, see what it's like to remember that distressed and overwhelmed perspectives are not necessarily a reflection of poor theology. Instead, these are a road map to spaces inside that are in need of tender care. Remember the embedded beliefs we looked at in chapter 4? We want to keep these in mind, gently considering how they might be at play in our reactions.

Rather than trying to force ourselves to get to a state of safety and stay there, we're going to take our time making sense of the muscle memory that shapes how we currently move through our autonomic terrain. If we can understand the perspectives that parts of us hold in these states, we can more helpfully locate what the depths of our soul need when we're cycling through stress or shutdown, unable to anchor in a sense of safety.

PAUSE & PLAY:

MAPPING OUR AUTONOMIC LANDSCAPE

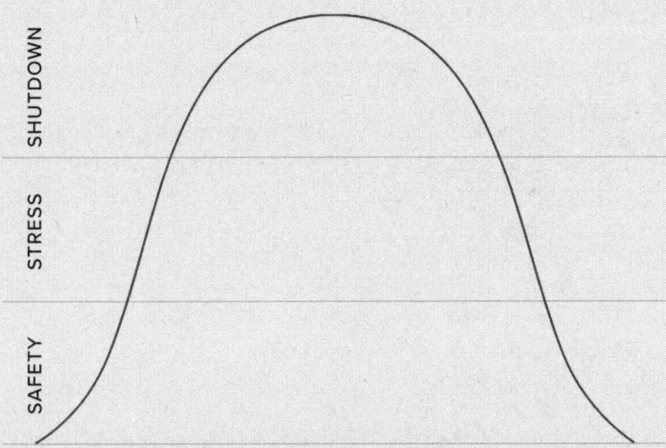

On a piece of paper, draw two horizontal lines to create three sections. On the bottom, write *Safety*, in the middle write *Stress*, and on the top write *Shutdown*.[8] In each section, create some sort of depiction of what life is like when you are in that state of safety, stress, and shutdown. You can draw and write anything that matches how you experience each state.

For example, you might include depictions of weather, landscape, animals, relationships, or any other symbols that illustrate your gut level associations with each of these three states. If you don't have access to paper at this moment, let your mind sketch out the different ways you experience these three states.

Next, consider how you see the world when your body is anchored in safety, activated in stress, or overwhelmed in shutdown. How is your perspective connected to what's happening in your body in each of these states?

Reflect on each of the following:

How do I see other people when I'm in a state of ____________ (safety/stress/shutdown)?

For example, "I see other people as distant or unable to help me when I'm in a state of shutdown."

How do I view myself when I'm in a state of ___________________ *(safety/stress/shutdown)?*

For example, "I see myself as messing things up when I'm in a state of stress."

How do I see God when I'm in a state of _____________________ *(safety/stress/shutdown)?*

For example, "I don't see God anywhere when I'm in a state of shutdown."

CHAPTER 7

tuning in with internal reactions

Let's go back into the mountains with that massive, beautiful black bear. As I stood next to Sarah, I was painfully aware of the contrast between the volume of her voice and the silence of my own. In my mind, I kept thinking, *I need to yell. That is our best chance of scaring the bear away.* No matter how many times I told myself this, I just couldn't figure out how to make it happen.

Internally it felt like an engine was revving, ready to burst into action any second, as though my body was shouting, *Come on! Let's go!* At the same time, as my muscles and jaw stayed locked shut, another part of me sang a different tune, shouting, *FREEZE! DON'T SPEAK! DON'T MOVE!* I was activated by my internal gas pedal, which fueled me with adrenaline, and at the same time I'd been stopped in my tracks, immobilized by my internal brake system.

And then, the part of me that wanted to yell eventually got out one pitiful yelp, a tiny noise that didn't compare with the volume or tone of Sarah's voice. After this, it was like the part of me that wanted to stay small and quiet demanded that I not make another noise, silencing my voice as Sarah yelled for both of us. In those moments, the internal push-pull made clear that my thinking brain was not in the driver's seat. Instead, other parts of me were in control, trying to help me get back to safety at an instinctual gut level. They just had different ideas about how to do this best.

And so I stood there, silent and stuck.

Protective Strategies

Our body is wired with a number of protective strategies designed to help us navigate stress and danger so that we can move through life as safely as possible.[1] These protective reactions operate across autonomic states, using the internal gas pedal and brake system to bring our body back into a felt sense of safety. We can think of these movements as parts of us functioning protectively to safeguard what is vulnerable within, the spaces inside that have been shaped by times we didn't experience the sense of safety we needed.

When these protective strategies take the driver's seat, it can sometimes feel as if we're working against ourselves in our attempts to move toward safety, especially when our body moves against the logic of our thinking brain. This goes back to neuroception—the way our body scans for threat or danger, trying to determine if we're safe. When our body perceives that we are not secure—physically, emotionally, or otherwise—we'll draw on various movements that have become intertwined with parts of us. You've probably heard of at least three of these movements: fight, flight, or freeze.

When we pick up a cue of danger or stress, our body sometimes decides that fighting is our best option.[2] We often associate this response with a physical threat like a tiger or bear—a situation where we might literally need to fight for our life. This very same instinct can also surge beneath the surface whenever our body picks up certain relational and emotional cues that we perceive as threatening. We might experience this *fight* energy in ourselves or another person who gets snippy or argumentative at work, or with someone we live with! When this happens, it might seem like the person is looking for a fight, but really, something inside them sensed a perceived attack or slight, and in response, they're reactively guarding themselves with a fight instinct. When we experience this in another person, it can sometimes feel like we're experiencing *another side of them*. Really what we're often seeing is a version of themselves that has been activated by a stress state—a part that is moved by a *protective strategy* to fight.

Sometimes our body instead decides that *flight*—getting away from or out of a situation—is our best option. A small example of this happens when we instinctively pull our hand back from a hot stovetop. As our hand retreats from the heat, our body is fleeing or moving away from perceived danger. In relational contexts, fleeing might look like walking away in the middle of an argument or emotionally withdrawing when we can't physically leave a space.

Along with the better known fight-or-flight reactions, our body might choose other protective strategies, such as *fawn* and *find*,[3] to try to get back to safety. When we fawn, we submit or engage in people-pleasing, trying not to rock the boat. We fawn when we sense that the best way to move through stress is to get small and quiet and not cause a problem. This might look like agreeing with someone in an attempt to avoid conflict—or to keep from making an existing conflict any worse.

Similarly, when we find under stress, we seek out connection from another person or group, like a pack. We'll instinctively attempt to find when our body senses that we can't get through a stressor alone and that we need to attach to another person for protection or comfort. This might look like calling a friend, asking a loved one to hold us, or sheltering in a community of people who can give us a sense of—or actual—protection. Since a sense of safety is so deeply intertwined with interpersonal connection, it's no mystery that we might reach or grasp for others as we try to make our way back to safety, hoping it might anchor and shelter us.

If we experience extreme distress, our bodies might feel paralyzed and *freeze*, collapse and *flop*, or disconnect and *fragment*. When we respond in any of these ways, we are no longer purely in stress but have crossed over into the territory of shutdown. At this point, our body is simply trying to survive whatever we're experiencing, whether physically or emotionally. You can imagine freeze as a deer in the headlights, both standing tall with the energy of the gas pedal and standing still with a foot on the brakes. You can envision flop as the response of someone who has passed out on a drop tower at an amusement park, and fragment as an out-of-body experience. When we freeze, our muscles feel rigid and paralyzed. When we flop, our muscles give out. When we fragment, we might not feel connected to the muscles in our own body, and instead might feel as though we're watching ourselves from outside our body.

While we might get frustrated by the ways our body moves through the muscle memory of protective strategies, it's important to remember: These reactions come from our body's innate wisdom and are designed to help keep us safe. Each of the responses listed above—fight, flight, fawn, find, freeze, flop, and fragment[4]—happens instinctively before our thinking brain puts together a strategic plan. While it might seem strange to think about our body strategizing below conscious thought, it's really a brilliant design—like an automatic, built-in system that moves us away from danger and threats and toward safety and security.

As we discover how we tend to move through these strategies, it's important to remember that none is more noble or flawed than any other. Depending on how we are wired and what experiences we have walked through, we will move through certain protective strategies most frequently.

On the day Sarah and I encountered the bear, different parts of me had different ideas of what the best protective strategy would be. While my thinking brain could get on board with the protective strategy of getting into a fight posture—to get big and loud—another part of me could not. It didn't matter that I knew what I was "supposed" to do. This other part of me was terrified, feeling helpless to bring myself back to a baseline of safety. As my body pressed on both the brakes and the gas, I could sense my system stalling near shutdown, leaving my body unable to shout and barely able to move.

That afternoon, the conflict in my body resolved pretty easily: We heard the rustling of fresh fall leaves crunching beneath the bear's paws as he scurried off. After hearing nothing but silence for a good while,

Sarah and I cautiously turned the corner again. We sheepishly crept ahead and felt better when we were a good half mile or so down the trail. The internal tension dissolved as I continued to put one foot in front of the other on the dirt path ahead of me, feeling the breeze against my face and gazing out on a valley surrounded by tree-blanketed mountains. It was an ideal environment for my body to regulate after distress.

While that bear makes for a good story, encounters with wildlife are the exception rather than the norm of experiences that prompt our bodies to be moved by protective strategies. So what happens when the external cue sending us into varying degrees of stress and shutdown doesn't run off into the woods?

PAUSE & PLAY:

PROTECTIVE PERSPECTIVES

As we explore protective strategies, I'm curious to know what you might be noticing stirring within. Did you feel a tightness in your neck or defensiveness in your gut after reading any of the examples? Did past experiences or conflicts with loved ones float up to the surface? Before you continue, take a moment to simply notice any thoughts, emotions, bodily sensations, and memories that have come up during this chapter so far. Remember, at any moment, you can pause and spend time with the grounding exercises on pages 24–25 to *be with* what's stirring within.

To get to know our protective strategies better, we're going to try to see the world through the eyes of each perspective that's embedded in a reaction to fight, flight, fawn, find, freeze, flop, and fragment. Each statement below represents the instinctual body logic of one of these strategies. As you read through the list, see what it's like to consider these perspectives as trains of thought that are anchored at a gut level within our neuroception—our body's perception of whether or not we're safe.

Fight: If I confront what's in front of me, I can tackle it and this will be over. Then I can breathe again. *The body is fueled to battle through a stressor.*

Flight: If I run away or get away from what's in front of me, I won't have to deal with it anymore. Then I can breathe again. *The body is fueled to move away.*

Fawn: If I keep my mouth shut and don't rock the boat, this will all be over sooner. Then I can breathe again. *The body is fueled and activated by stress while also using the brakes to move cautiously as needed.*

Find: If I reach out to someone who can protect me or comfort me, I'll be okay. Then I can breathe again. *The body is fueled to move toward another person or group.*

Freeze: There's nothing I can do. I can't find a way to make it through this and breathe again. *The body is stuck in the tension of being both fueled and stopped, feeling paralyzed.*

Flop: There's nothing I can do. I'm entirely overwhelmed. I can't find a way to make it through this and breathe again. *The body gives out and goes limp.*

Fragment: There's nothing I can do. I can't find a way to make it through this and breathe again. Being here is absolutely intolerable. *The body disconnects and dissociates from the present.*

Now, read through the list again. As you do, see if you can let your mind play out scenes in which you imagine these protective strategies as versions of yourself, animals, caricatures, or TV characters.

Notice how you imagine the embodiment of these protective strategies. How do they move? What else might they say? How would they fill out a body-outline worksheet to describe the emotions in their bodies?

Mountains of Stress

Let's step away from the trail where I encountered that bear and look at the Smoky Mountains from a distance. When you're far away from them, they look like a sea of blue and purple layers, fading into the distance. Their tree-blanketed ridges are both soft and strong, changing colors each season. But every time my mom refers to the Smokies as what they are—mountains—a certain niece and nephew of mine are confused.

These sweet little nuggets have grown up in the Pacific Northwest, seeing Mount Baker behind them and the Canadian Rockies in the distance nearly every day. They regularly spend their weekends hiking or snowshoeing through the Northern Cascades. To them, those are mountains, stunning snow-covered rock that tower above 10,000 feet. In their daily lives, my niece and nephew are surrounded by landscape marked by distinct and dramatic distances between sea level and the peaks of these world-class mountains.

When they visit family in Tennessee, they're perplexed. As they ride around town with their grandma, my mom points excitedly whenever the Smoky Mountains come into view. She asks, "Do you see the mountains?" She's thrilled to share the beauty of the mountains that she grew up visiting and still cherishes. A tender part of her gets excited when she sees their glorious blue layers pop up in the horizon, and she wants to share in that joy with her precious grandchildren.

In response to their grandma's question, my niece and nephew furrow their little brows and look out the windows, confused. One of them will point a little finger toward the horizon and say, "No, where are they? I only see those hills!" Even when Mount LeConte, towering at 6,593 feet, is visible in the sea of blue-ridged foothills, these little ones don't see any mountains. They only see hills.

They're not being pretentious. They're making sense of the world around them based on what they have known. And what they know is living at sea level while surrounded by mountains that stand 10,000 feet and taller. Their bodies know the long and windy roads they travel to get to these heights.

And so the tree-covered Smokies don't look at all like mountains to them. It makes complete sense that no matter how much we kindly try to help them understand that what they're seeing in Tennessee are indeed mountains, they're not convinced.

This imagery can help us play with mapping out elevations of stress in our life. Set in a different order from the visual we looked at in the last chapter, here we can consider another way of looking at how we move through the terrain of safety, stress, and shutdown. In this imagery, sea level represents a place where we are grounded and experiencing little to no stress, varying degrees of higher elevations represent different levels of stress, and the depths of the sea represent our experience of sinking into shutdown. And depending on the metaphoric elevation we are in, we're likely to find ourselves moved by protective strategies intended to help us survive those heights or depths.[5]

If you have hiked above 6,000 feet of elevation, you know that the air is thinner there than when you're hiking at 4,000 feet. When you're closer to sea level, you can breathe more deeply. Now, say the lowest elevation our body is used to moving through in a stress state is a metaphorical 4,000 feet above sea level. In this case, it's possible that our body's sense of descending into a full and gentle stop at sea level will be conditioned by the exposure to higher elevation, and we'll mistake the side of a mountain for the side of the sea. And if we're used to sinking into the depths of survival or shutdown, we may mistake a sense of treading water for freely floating on the water's surface or basking in the sun by the shoreline.

The muscle memory of the protective strategies that move us through various elevations is often deeply engrained in us, shaping the movements of different parts of us as they take the driver's seat. And if this muscle memory feels normal to us, we often won't have a frame of reference to help us see how far off our baseline elevation actually is from sea level. Like my sweet niece and nephew, our perspectives are shaped by the reference points we know. Tragically, when parts of us have been conditioned to help us survive high elevations, deep sea depths, or both, our perception of what safety feels like can become distorted.

When I think back on the push-pull in my body when I first started to tune in with what was happening inside, I realize I didn't entirely long for life to move more slowly. I would have said that I liked how fast-paced my days were, and I wasn't interested in slowing down. This was because I didn't know there were freer or more flexible movements I could move through that would have grounded me at more steady elevations. I thought the protective strategies my body knew were just part of regular life. I didn't recognize that parts of me were cycling through fight and fawn, or when I was pushed too far, another part would nearly flop before the gas pedal would fuel some fight in me again.

Because my body was used to high peaks of stress, it was easy for me to mistake lower peaks of stress for a different autonomic state. I misinterpreted the sense of relief I felt at a lower elevation as a sign I was out of a stress state when in reality I was still in the mountains—the landscape just looked different. I had to slow down and get to know the flora and fauna of varying elevations to map out where I actually was in a stress state. There was also a whole new landscape and terrain at sea level to explore.

Tumbling Down

Remember that morning I collapsed in a puddle of tears on my bathroom floor?

If my body could have spoken in that moment, I think she would have said, "I have nothing left! I cannot breathe, I cannot sleep, I cannot keep *going*. Pressing the gas pedal is no longer an option. Continuing to hike up this never-ending 30,000-foot mountain is not an option. I must stop. I cannot keep fighting, I cannot keep fawning. No more gas pedal and brakes fighting each other. I'm overriding the gas and putting a cement block on the brakes."

When my body collapsed, I felt as though all of me was tumbling down from high elevations of stress before hitting some rocks and bouncing into the sea, where I sank to the ocean floor. It was not a gentle or gradual descent but as abrupt as slamming the brakes into immediate shutdown. My body didn't know how to gently press the brakes in that season, so an abrupt shutdown was the only option my body was able to navigate that day.

As I was curled up in a ball on the ground, my body made clear I needed to learn to move through elevations of life in a way that wouldn't require my body to force a strenuous climb or to tumble down to a painful stop.

When I reflected on that day, initially a part of me wanted to reduce what was happening inside to simple categories. I thought, *All right, high peaks of stress are bad, and the lows of shutdown are also bad. I need to figure out how to live right in the midst of a sweet spot—regardless of all the variables of weather, seasons, other hikers, and wildlife around. I need to figure out how to stay perfectly* right there *in a little zone of safety*. This kind of goal was of course not helpful, let alone possible.

What I actually needed was a way to place an anchor at sea level so that all parts of my embodied being could know what an autonomic state of safety feels like. But in order to find a new home here—or perhaps more accurately, become reacquainted with what was always intended to be my home—I needed to understand the stories that had shaped my time in the mountains and my sinking in the sea.

PAUSE & PLAY:

WHAT'S MY BASELINE?

Let's see what your body might have to tell you about the elevations you move through in life. Imagine having a conversation with your body, using the following prompts to facilitate some dialogue. Be curious to notice what it's like to tune in and listen to any way your body might be giving you feedback, whether it's through sensation, emotion, memory, mental imagery, or thoughts.

If it feels helpful, you can (1) draw or imagine this conversation like a cartoon using stick figures and speech bubbles to give voice to your body, (2) move between two empty chairs as you play the roles of your thinking brain and your body, or (3) go on a walk, imagining you're talking with your body as you would talk with a friend walking alongside you.

See what it's like to actively empathize, reflect back what you're hearing, and engage with your body in this conversation.

Questions to gently ask your body:

What do you want me to know about how you experience the mountain ranges of stress that we journey through?

What do you want me to know about how you experience the depths of the sea that sometimes make us feel as if we're sinking or drowning, unable to come up for air?

Do we consider our baseline to be a relaxed state (sea level), or is our baseline actually a low-level stress or shutdown state?

Is this what our baseline has always been? If not, how long has it been like this?

CHAPTER 8

tuning in with internal stories

I glanced at the clock as I drove, realizing there was no way I'd be on time for the coffee date I'd made with a friend. I was frustrated and stressed, and I wondered why I had yet again made more plans than I could feasibly commit to. I knew the limited hours in a day. I knew I had limited energy that could sustain me for only so long. I knew how many hours I needed to sleep at night. How did I keep getting the math wrong? No matter how often I vowed not to schedule extra work or other commitments, I kept swimming through days with no margin, furious with no one but myself.

So now I was fuming internally, knowing that in the midst of a busy day in the midst of a stressful week, I had overscheduled myself *again*. Agitated, I couldn't be fully present with the friend I was meeting, or the work I'd tend to afterward. The muscle memory I was cycling in was no longer working for me. Feeling stuck, I wasn't interested in slowing down or getting curious—I just wanted to start getting the math right! In this equation, the problem was me, and I needed to get my act together.

Harsh, judgmental, self-critical parts of me don't like the idea of slowing down and getting curious about the story that shapes the protective strategies and muscle memory pushing me through life. Instead, these critical parts demand that I simply use my thinking brain to do better and change my behavior. The irony is that, for me, the reason these parts of me feel this way is because of the unwanted critical judgments that have been placed on them.

This self-shaming muscle memory seems to always be there, ready to pounce at any moment. She's like an additional watchdog that tries to keep me in line. And while it can feel as if this inner-critic guard dog is tearing me down with her barks and bites, when I've slowed down with this perspective, I've realized that just like many other gut reactions, she wants to help me. She believes she can keep me safe if by shaming me she can keep me from getting curious. From her perspective, when I slow down and get vulnerable, I'm at greater risk for harm than when I just keep pushing through life, not connecting with what's happening beneath the surface. Her barks of shame are fueled by the gas pedal, keeping my body in the tension and rigidity of a stress state, unable to yield into the flexibility or openness of safety.

I've lost count of the number of times that a client has looked at me in disbelief, annoyance, or even anger after I've gently asked whether a part of them that seems to be complicating their life might actually be trying to help them. And this makes sense—getting curious about how a protective strategy might be trying to help us can sometimes feel like letting an angry dog bite our hand off as we curiously wonder, *How might you be trying to help me?*

When we're convinced that something or someone is causing trouble, even if we believe the problem is a part of us, we're not likely to be amused if someone suggests that this supposed critic has good intentions. Such a suggestion can reasonably feel unhelpful and even dismissive.

Whether it's the version of us that's once again late to the coffee date, the inner critic[1] that tells us how flawed we are, or the skeptical part of us that doesn't believe therapy techniques can help us, we can better understand the different facets of ourselves when we approach their perspectives with curiosity and compassion.

Mindful of the complexities that inner critics and self-shame bring to the table, we're going to start piecing together what we've been exploring in the first two parts of the book. As we do this, I want to name that it's completely normal to face internal resistance when trying to get to know certain facets of ourselves. One of the most constructive antidotes to this tension is simply slowing down with curiosity—something we've been doing with each Pause & Play.

PAUSE & PLAY:

GETTING TO KNOW A PART

Let's slow down and get curious about a specific part of us that has popped up while reading the first seven chapters.[2] Approaching the muscle memory that lives inside us with curiosity can help us notice things we normally wouldn't see, gaining a more holistic picture of what shapes the protective strategies that move us through life.

Look over the graphic below, which depicts the different strands we're stringing together based on what we've looked at in the previous chapters.

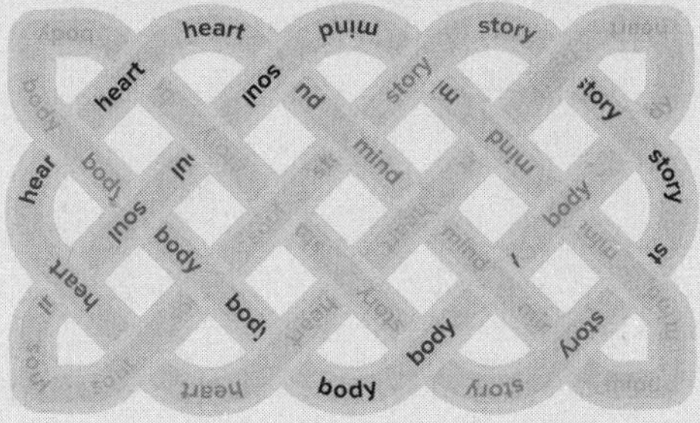

Before surveying the following list, bring to mind a specific part of you that you can't make sense of or that often frustrates you. This might be the part of you that resonates with the annoyance you feel toward yourself when you're late for a coffee date. This might be the version of you that feels like you freeze in conflict. Maybe it's the side of you that engages in people-pleasing at work or with loved ones. For now, consider connecting with something that isn't too heavy, honoring that something connected to a trauma or deep wound might be overwhelming to start with.

Once you have this part of yourself in mind, slowly ask yourself the following questions. If at any time you notice that you feel judgmental rather than curious, ask the judgments if they would be willing to step aside to allow you some space to try this exercise. If at any time you feel overwhelmed or triggered, consider taking a step back and engaging in one of the grounding practices offered at the beginning of the book.

Reflect back to chapter 2: *Do I notice a resistance to slowing down and getting in touch with what's happening inside? In what ways does this feel risky, threatening, or inconvenient?*

Reflect back to chapter 3: *What's going on in my body when this part of me shows up? How would I fill in a body outline worksheet to depict what's happening inside? Which emotions would be present, and how would they be represented in my body?*

Reflect back to chapter 4: *If my internal world were a house, where would this part of me live? Forgotten, locked away behind closed doors? Clawing at a door to get out? Silently staying in the dark, having given up? Do I view this part of me as bad, thinking they need to get in line spiritually or any other way?*

Reflect back to chapter 5: *When I consider this part of me, do I feel the gas and/or the brakes pressed inside? Do I feel a surge of anxiety or stress? Do I feel stopped in my tracks or like I'm going to explode or crumble? Are the movements abrupt or subtle? Fueled or flattened?*

Reflect back to chapter 6: *Where in the autonomic landscape does this part of me tend to live (safety, stress, or shutdown)? Is it just one state, or a mixture of two or more? How does this part move in or through this terrain?*

Reflect back to chapter 7: *Which protective strategies (fight, flight, fawn, freeze, find, flop, fragment) do I feel move this part of me and shape their perspective? At what elevations of safety, stress, or shutdown do these protective strategies move me through?*

TUNING IN WITH INTERNAL STORIES

As you consider the reflections you've pieced together so far, ask yourself the following:

When I imagine this part of me as a person, how would I describe them?

Are they a version of me? Are they a cartoon character or animal? Are they some sort of symbolic imagery?

What's their facial expression like? What's their body posture like? What are their movements like?

How old does this part of me feel? Do they feel my age today, or does their perspective feel younger? What age or age range would I link them with?

And once you have an image in your mind of this part of you, imagine asking them:

What do you want me to see and know about your perspective, about your movements? What things am I misunderstanding or judging too quickly?

Can you help me understand how you're trying to help me?

Can you help me understand what you are scared of or trying to avoid? What past wounds that shape your perspective would you like me to honor or tend toward?

Tapping into Story

I'll be the first to admit that it's not initially obvious that seemingly problematic parts of us might be trying to be helpful.[3] The more disconnected I was from what was happening beneath my thinking brain, the more likely I was to see parts of me, and their autonomic muscle memory, as problems. Tuning out what was happening deep down made it all the easier for my inner critic to judge and criticize the protective strategies that parts of me would move through. Without thinking, I would scapegoat them for complicating my life.

In the case of my tendency to overschedule my days with extra work hours and social commitments, I was exhausting myself without making time to recharge. I saw no solution other than getting it together by using my thinking brain to force behavior modification tactics. I just needed to manage my schedule better—it was that simple.

I'd get angry with myself, wondering, *What's wrong with me? Why do I keep doing this? I know better!* I'd specifically resent the "me" that said yes and made these plans. Then one day, I realized that when I was making plans or saying yes to them, parts of me were often either fawning or finding. There was a part of me that didn't want to say no and strain a relationship or cause someone else to be upset. There was also a part of me that knew what it felt like to be alone and didn't want to miss out on an opportunity to strengthen a relational connection. She was reaching for connection in a way that was fueled by stress—in fear of disconnect—rather than from an anchored place of calm and rest.

When I was growing up, my dad's company transferred him frequently, so we moved every couple of years in and outside of the United States. I cycled between four different elementary schools in three different countries. Being the new kid over and over in foreign spaces cultivated a muscle memory that made making friends feel a bit like a survival game. I knew what it felt like to walk into a new space small and alone, knowing no one, unsure of whether I would feel this way for the entire school year. And so, during those years, parts of me did everything they could to make and avoid losing friends, bracing for loss when we would move. It was exhausting to know each time wouldn't be the last time I'd have to start the whole process over again.

During those young years, my body learned to press on the gas, fueled by fear and uncertainty as I tried to navigate the new group of classmates in front of me. Simultaneously, a part of me attempted to appear normal and not stressed, keeping my activation locked inside. My body became used to shifting through life and relationships in a high gear of stress, holding that pressure internally so it would hopefully not interfere with my external relationships. All of this swirled beneath my conscious awareness.

I now realize it was difficult to gently press on the brakes or yield into a sense of security in relationships when I knew we would soon have to move again. The one time I remember settling into a sense of predictability was when I was ten. My dad had been told that his company would keep us in one location for fifteen years. That meant I could finish elementary school, middle school, and high school in the same place after already having attended three elementary schools across two countries.

Then his company merged with another. My parents told us we would be moving to the Netherlands—or as my sister and I first referred to it, the Neverlands. We were devastated to leave the United States after just having moved back. Our oldest sister, who was starting her freshman year of college, would stay stateside, no longer a short four hours away from us.

We knew that this move, like all the others, was temporary. Even though I wasn't aware of it at the time, I now see the ways my body feared having a sense of security ripped away again. And so my body spent those three years in the Netherlands revving the gas pedal every morning, filling my body with so much anxiety that I would feel sick to my stomach before going to school. I carried this anxiety with me all day long, becoming desensitized to the amount of stress coursing through my body in regular life.

For years this was just my normal, not something I ever considered approaching with curiosity, compassion, or empathy. It was only when I received the warmth of curiosity and compassion from others that I decided it might be worth tending to the pain that these parts of me had experienced and carried for so long. Along the way, I realized that these parts of me still felt only eleven years old, walking alone into a new school in a new country, with just her little purple backpack on her shoulders.

Regardless of our age, we carry with us every version of ourselves from younger years. In a fascinatingly mysterious way, we are both the same person and a different person from who we were at the ages of one, five, ten, and twenty. And plenty of cues in life, whether it be a certain smell, memory, holiday, or relationship, can bring us right back to each of these ages.

Now when I'm frustrated with myself for seemingly not thinking and overscheduling, I recognize more of the puzzle pieces that explain why I had agreed to activities I simply didn't have energy for. I can gently and kindly remind these younger parts of me of things that in the past I would have tried to address only with shame and behavior modification.

When I'm tempted to agree to social plans I know I won't have margin for, I can remind eleven-year-old me that I am no longer in the vulnerable circumstance of having to move with my dad's job. I can let her know that she is not alone, being curious to see if she finds comfort in my presence or in God's presence holding her. I can start to address her anxieties, helping her know that it's not her job to make everyone happy, and that she will be safe and secure even if someone is upset that I said no to their plans. I can also let her know that as an adult I have more autonomy and choice in how I cultivate friendships. As a result, I don't have to overschedule myself to ensure that I won't feel alone. Friendships are no longer a survival game like they were for that little girl.

Just as I picked up Bashful and held her close to make sure she *knew* she was no longer in the dark room alone, I play with how to invite this part of me into an embrace to help her know that we're no longer back there—that we're here, and we're safe.

Moving toward this part of me did not magically happen in one therapy session or while listening to one podcast. For so long, my posture toward this part of me was shaped by my inner critic. From this critic's perspective, there wasn't space for curiosity or to consider the story that had shaped this autonomic muscle memory. From her perspective, the only solution was to shame myself again and again, which in the moment seemed constructive but in the long run, kept me stuck.

This sticky self-shame that fuels our inner critic often feels like one of the biggest barriers to exploring new muscle memory. Rather than trying to bypass the inner critic or simply asking them to step back, we can notice when their perspective is the loudest and then listen to them, reassuring them that *we are on the same team.*

While we might not be able to tangibly pick up the parts of us that live inside, we can hold them with our curiosity, compassion, kindness, and empathy, feeling *with* them, weeping *with* them, and seeing them as we hold our body, which might look like placing a hand over our heart, or wrapping our arms around our torso or legs.

Getting Curious

The image of eleven-year-old me with a little purple backpack, anxiously uncertain as she walks into a new school, might feel like a sweet picture to attach to the muscle memory that moved me through life. What about the not-so-pretty pictures that are neither cute nor sweet?

Getting curious feels especially sticky when we consider the parts of us that seem to drive how we handle conflict with loved ones. When I first heard someone suggest that parts of us always have some sort of logic for how they're trying to help us, I couldn't help but wonder, *How in the world could a fiery part of me that easily gets fully charged into fighting and reacts by getting snippy, sarcastic, unkind, and demeaning be trying to help me?*

As a marriage counselor, I knew that this part of me contributed to negative cycles[4] that never helped my relationships, especially with my husband. Even though I'd been able to track the movements of those negative cycles, I felt helpless to make changes once I found myself in them. As soon as my heart started to beat faster, my voice would rise louder, and my facial muscles would contort to display anger and contempt.

From my point of view, I just wanted to get rid of this part of me that was getting in the way of peace in my relationship. It took an elixir of curiosity from my spiritual director and therapist for me to even consider that maybe, just maybe, there was more happening beneath the surface that was worth getting curious about. From their compassionate points of view, maybe there was a part of me reacting beneath the awareness of my thinking brain who felt threatened by the conflict and was trying to keep me feeling safe.

When I joined with their curiosity, I started to understand the old story that this part of me was still moving through, trying to protect me. In another relationship, I was made to feel as small as possible whenever there was conflict. In those spaces, the most vulnerable depths of me were mistreated and harmed over and over again, which eventually prompted protective strategies to emerge to help me get through those conflicts and never have to feel that kind of pain again. And despite being in a relationship with a different person in the present, these parts of me operated from a muscle memory that associated conflict with the need to gear up into a protective strategy to try to fight my way through it.

The very moment my body sensed conflict outside me, it would inform my neuroception that the present circumstance didn't feel safe or good. And then, at a gut level, the associations of earlier conflict—when I'd been mistreated and demeaned—would also pop up.

The muscle memory inside me would then push forward a part of me that saw the world as a place I needed to fight through, a place where I would feel small, alone, and helpless if I didn't fend for myself. And so that part of me would function protectively, pressing on the gas. My muscle memory was trying to take care of vulnerable depths within me that had been injured earlier in my life, guarding them from feeling the pain that my body remembered in these moments.

Once I understood how this part of me saw the world, based on the old story that she thought she was still living in, I could move toward her, tending to the fear and wounds that were pressing in on her. I could slow down and bring this part of me into the present, letting her know that we are no longer in the past where she needed to fight. I could thank her for how fiercely she wanted to protect the vulnerable depths of me that had been so deeply hurt, and I could invite her into a new role that would allow her to move more freely. She now had the choice to move differently, something that was nearly disorienting.

And from this place, I could enter conflict differently. To be clear: This did not happen immediately nor does it mean that I handle conflict perfectly—just ask my husband! But what's different in the midst of cycles of conflict is that the parts of me that move underneath my thinking brain now know that I have choices for how I move through conflict—that I am safe and don't have to fight in the ways I used to. I'm now in a relationship with a different person who treats me differently. In other words, from both vulnerable and protective perspectives internally, I can now see and move through the story of the present rather than feeling stuck in and moved by the stories of the past.

It's incredibly important to pause here and say that getting curious about the stories that shape our lives does not give us license to harm others. Instead, in its most restorative form, getting curious can be a vulnerable exploration of what's happening within that leads us to spaces that are in need of healing—healing that might even extend to those around us.

As we tune in with the stories that shape how different parts of us move through protective strategies, we can trace what's going on beneath the surface. This gives us a road map to discover where we can tend toward inside, or more precisely, *who* to tend toward inside. This is entirely different from trying to force parts of us into behavior modification and cognitive restructuring.

When we take time to see the world through the eyes of parts of us, we can trace the logic of their protective and vulnerable viewpoints. We can also empathize with how these parts of us see the world so that we, in turn, can help them feel seen, heard, and understood. This kind of genuine connection is necessary if we want to take risks to move through life differently, cultivating a new muscle memory that is anchored in the present rather than being moved by old muscle memory that is stuck in the past. Until they are seen, heard, and understood, parts of us are likely to feel like perpetual problems rather than facets of our created being.

As we continue to connect with what's happening inside, we'll now turn to exploring ways we might tend to and care for our internal landscape. But first, let's spend a little more time learning the stories that shape our movements.

PAUSE & PLAY:

LEARNING THE STORY

Think back to the part of you that you were focusing on in the first Pause & Play of this chapter. Consider a specific real-life example of how this part of you can frustrate or annoy you, or in some other way feel like a problem. Again, I encourage you not to focus on anything that is too heavy or triggering as you begin to connect with parts of yourself.

Once you have a specific scenario in mind of how this part can frustrate or annoy you, or seemingly complicate your life, reflect on the story this part of you carries as you move through the following prompts:

Imagine placing the pen in the hand of this part of you, asking them to write their story. What would they say? Beyond considering your gut reaction to this question, take time to sit down and write, seeing what words this part of you might want to share.

If you sense a mental or emotional block when trying to engage with this exercise, rather than trying to force anything, consider pausing and noticing what's happening in your body (thoughts, emotions, body sensations, memories). You can pause with your hand over your heart and ask yourself, *Is there something about this exercise that's just too risky right now?*

If it feels difficult to connect with words, consider inviting this part of you to draw a picture book to tell their story. Be curious to notice if any ideas for a picture book are similar to stories you read as a child. Is there something about the artwork or themes of these books that resonates with the story that this part of you wants you to see and hear?

If at any moment, you notice that an inner critic or another part of you wants their voice and story to be heard, consider pausing and coming up with a plan for these different parts of you to each take a turn. See what it's like to let each part of you know that this will allow you to learn their different points of view.

This might look like imagining that you are addressing two or three people who are all trying to talk to you at once, asking them to pause as you can only hear and respond to them one at a time. See if these parts of you are willing to take turns, reassuring each of them that you will take time to honor their voice and listen to their story (so long as this feels genuine to your posture toward them).

As you listen to the stories that you hold within, notice how the points of view in the narratives are similar to or different from how you tend to view things. See what it's like to imagine living life through their perspective.

PART THREE

tend to the depths of the soul

CHAPTER 9

tending to what's been forgotten

Over the last few years, I've had the joy of watching two of my husband's siblings welcome foster children into their families. Seeing them open their homes and their arms to these precious little girls has been one of the most beautiful demonstrations of love I've ever witnessed. One of these nieces came into my brother- and sister-in-law's home after being severely neglected. This sweet girl was also born addicted to drugs, and because she had spent the majority of her first months stuck in a car seat, she was unable to crawl or hold herself up.

Her new brothers loved having her around, and I watched my husband's brother and his wife truly take her in as one of their own. Early on, she would often be on the hip of her new foster mom, not responding to tone or facial expressions, seemingly just going with the flow.

When Elijah and I first met her, she was unresponsive to our smiles and other attempts to engage with her. Having enjoyed the role of being an aunt for many years, I'd try my hardest to connect with her when I saw her, but no games of peekaboo, flashy toys, or playfulness would prompt her to respond. When we greeted her or said goodbye, it was as though she didn't hear us. She didn't make the slightest acknowledgement of hearing our voices or her name spoken. I wasn't sure if I should give up or keep trying to bridge the disconnect.

Then one night at a family gathering, I noticed something was different. I was chatting with my sister-in-law Ally as my little niece was resting securely on her hip. After a minute or so, I saw her look up at Ally, seeking out her gaze.

I was struck. I had never seen this niece look at someone with that kind of connectedness before. Along with her eyes reaching out for contact, I saw the muscles of her mouth move into the shape of a smile, something else I had never seen her do. And then as her face sought out Ally's face, my niece reached her little fingers toward her as well. She then began to bounce her entire little being, like she was gearing up for a response. The movement of her whole body shouted with playfulness, "Come on! Play the game!"

My sister-in-law responded, mirroring the little smile and silliness that was reaching out to her. Her brown eyes lit up with the little brown eyes looking up at her. In harmony with her eyes, Ally's whole face was glowing, matching the smile that was inviting her to *be with* her in this moment. And to complete the whole interaction, she met the little fingers reaching for her, grasping them and holding this precious girl a little tighter. Just for a moment time seemed suspended as they waited for what would come next. Then in a rhythm they clearly both knew, Ally bounced up and down. Their bodies moved together, wiggling in playful laughter that they savored together.

As I watched this sweet girl come alive, I felt as if I was witnessing a sacred healing. Over and over again, I saw my niece seek out Ally, moving all the little muscles in her face to *play* their game of finding each other and sharing a connected moment. It was clear she felt a sense of security, *knowing* that as she played this game, my sister-in-law would respond. During the months she had spent in her foster home, her body had learned that she was not alone and was no longer neglected. Her body *knew* that she was seen and heard and that she would be held.

And then when we all sat down to eat, I noticed something else. Rather than sitting silently in her high chair, she started to make gestures and noises I hadn't heard before. As Ally offered her a bite of potatoes, she shook her head, pushing her little hands against the plastic spoon offered to her. Her voice squealed in protest, refusing the rest of her dinner.

Ally later said to all of us, "Even though it makes days harder, I'm so grateful for how she's pushing back now in ways that she never did before." She explained, "When she was first with us, she used to just go with the flow no matter what I did, so it wasn't as stressful for me to manage life with her and the boys.

"Now that she's made so much progress, she pushes back in the way a two-year-old normally would. And while that's frustrating in one way, I know it means that she's developing, which is a good thing. It makes meals and other moments more stressful for me, but it's so worth it knowing what that means—she's growing and she's healing."

An Invitation to Something New

Rather than seeing her foster daughter's behavior as a problem or something that had to be changed to make her own life more convenient, Ally dignified and honored her little girl's embodied being, exuding so much love, grace, and patience. She saw the bigger picture. As a mom to two older boys, she knew it was typical for a toddler to get frustrated at mealtime or when stuck in a high chair. What human wouldn't be frustrated if they didn't get a say in their dinner while being restrained in a chair?

The loud cries from this girl's tiny body meant that she felt safe in her circumstances and was now engaging differently with the world around her. Rather than being unresponsive in a state of learned helplessness, she could start to explore the world differently.

When I reflect on Ally's tenderness toward this little one, it almost feels like honey oozing down beneath my thinking brain, warming my heart and the depths of my soul. Watching their relationship play out, I can't help but wonder: What might it be like if we were to extend steady and gracious care to the parts of us that seem like problems? What if we tried mirroring God's own lovingkindness—care that isn't solely concerned with our behavior, but instead, sees the whole of who we are, delighting in our growth and our healing?

Reflecting on their interactions felt like an invitation to consider new ways to extend a similar soothing balm of tenderness to the parts of me that are still struggling to unlearn messages from myself and others—messages like, *Be quiet. Don't cause problems. Your needs do not matter. Your wants do not matter either.*

PAUSE & PLAY:

HOLDING TIGHT

I'm curious: What stands out to you in the story on the previous pages?

When you think about a little child seeking out the gaze of her mother, smiling and giggling as they bounce together, what happens inside of you?

In what ways does this image feel sweet?

In what ways does this image stir up pain or sadness?

I wonder if any part of you that has felt forgotten or neglected would love to be held tight. Or maybe being held closely feels too risky for some parts of you, making you uncomfortable and vulnerable in a way that doesn't feel safe yet.

For just a minute or two, let's see what it's like to play with an experiential exercise to connect with forgotten or neglected parts of you. If it doesn't feel possible to act out this exercise, play with acting it out in the imagination of your mind.

Find something around your home that represents a part of you that resonates with feeling forgotten or neglected. This item might be a pillow, a stuffed animal, a doll, a picture of you as a child, a plant, a figurine, a folded blanket, or anything else that you'd like to represent a part of you that has often been neglected.

After taking a deep breath or two, place the item that depicts this part of you somewhere in your home as a way to represent where this part lives inside you. Maybe it feels as if this part of you is hidden under a couch, stuffed inside a dresser drawer, thrown out on the back porch, kicked to the curb, locked behind a door, or sitting all alone in the middle of the floor. So long as it doesn't feel too distressing, place the item wherever it feels most fitting, even if your thinking brain can't make logical sense of the placement.

How does it feel to see a tangible depiction of this part of you? Be curious to feel the emotions that come up and then to observe how these emotions move through your body. Even if it's just for a moment, see what it's like to capture what's happening inside of you. If all you sense is that "nothing is happening inside," see what it's like to notice that nothing, being curious to explore if there are nuances of numbness or disconnection happening within.

Next, after another deep breath or two, be curious to consider how you feel toward this part of you and if you want to move toward them. If it feels genuine to do so, ask yourself how you might like to let this part of you know that you see them.

Even if it feels silly, try imagining telling this part of you, "I see you. You are not alone."

And if you'd like, as you speak words like this, notice what happens inside as you open a bridge of communication with this part of you.

Then if it feels genuine and safe to do so, take the deepest breath you've taken today and see what it's like to scoop the item up that's representing this part of you, remembering the imagery of me picking up Bashful who was alone in the dark bathroom.

You might first look at the item, playing out a conversation to ask this part of you if they want to be held, gently saying something like, "Is it okay if I pick you up?" or "Would you be open to me holding you?" If any other part of you reacts critically, telling you that this is ridiculous or stupid, see what it's like to ask this critical voice if they can give you some breathing room to try this exercise. With another deep breath you can see if this critical voice will take a step to the side, making way for you to try something new, watching what might happen.

And then pick up the item that you see as a forgotten part of you. See what it's like to hold the item tight, imagining that you are embracing this part of you. If it feels most fitting and safe, you can imagine this as a depiction of God holding this part of you. If that doesn't feel safe right now, don't force any spiritual integration.

As you play out holding this part of you, or if needed, holding space from this part of you, survey what's happening inside. Does this part of you want to be held like this, or held in any other way? Do you feel comfortable holding this part of you?

Read over the following and see if any of these thoughts resonate with longings you notice inside:

- Maybe this part of you wants to be wrapped against your body like an infant who is held close to her mother as she goes about her day.
- Maybe this part of you prefers to be like a little animal that gets to stay in your shirt pocket, a place they can nuzzle in, be close to you, and see what's happening in the world.
- Maybe this part of you pushes away, not ready for this kind of contact or engagement.
- Maybe this part of you needs a safe place to rest and heal, being tended to in the safety of a specific bedroom or home, real or imagined, where their needs are met and they are cared for while they regain their strength.
- Maybe this part of you wants to learn to use their little legs to walk alongside you, finding security by clutching your hands as they explore the world around them.
- Maybe this part of you wants to be carried on your hip, bouncing and clinging to your arm and the sound of your voice.

Take a minute to pause and breathe here, simply observing the gut reactions that are happening inside you. See if you can tune in with the voice of this part of you. If it feels difficult to respond with kindness or compassion, imagine responding to these longings if they came from another person or animal that you have nothing but love for.

You can play with this exercise more than once, and as you do, you can explore connection with different parts of yourself.

Exploring New Movements

Ally was spot-on when she observed that the little movements in front of her were part of a developmental process. From her foster daughter *yielding* so that she was fully resting her weight on Ally's hip, to her *pushing* back against a spoon offered her way, to her *reaching* for Ally's face or toys, to her *holding* and *pulling* them close, she was coming alive to movements that are inherent to us all.[1]

When we have everything we need to develop and grow in our first years of life, we initiate these kinds of movements naturally. Our sense of safety supports us as we explore the world and relationships in these ways.

Yielding simply means being in the world, feeling safe enough to blissfully be, letting all of our muscles relax and release. When we're able to yield, we don't feel the need to be doing anything. If we're yielding, we're not pressing on the gas pedal or slamming on the brakes. When we yield, we feel right at home as we are, calm and secure, held in the moment we're in. If we did not have the safety or support we needed to simply be when we were younger, it might be difficult for some parts of us to fully relax. They might confuse the stillness of yielding with being in a collapsed state, having never known what it was like to safely be supported and simply be.

From an anchored place of yielding, we can *push*. For example, infants push themselves into the movement of crawling, squirming away from a place they do not want to be. They might also push away a hand that tries to blow their nose or grab hold of their adorably plump cheeks. When we push from a grounded place of safety, we gain the flexibility to use the gas pedal or release the brakes for the energy that we need for particular movements.

When we push, we also explore independence and assert boundaries, movements that can be seen as problematic by caregivers. If they signaled to us that our autonomy was bad, we may be left without a muscle memory that knows that our needs and wants matter and that we have permission to move away from people and things that do not feel comfortable.

If we do have the support and safety we need to yield and push, we might also explore *reaching* for people and things around us. When we reach, we put ourselves in a vulnerable position. Reaching requires enough safety to be curious and take risks. When we reach toward another, we might be rejected, or we might be harmed in return. A curious child might reach out to a candle and be burned or to a busy parent and be shamed into being quiet.

When we reach from a place that is anchored in safety, we do not frantically press on the gas for this movement. Instead, we can freely gain momentum as we release the brakes—with or without a light tap on the gas pedal. In this case, the flexibility of how we move does not stem from stress but instead is grounded in safety.

Last but not least, *holding* and *pulling* are movements that build on yielding, pushing, and reaching. These are the riskiest of all movements, bringing what we reach for toward us and holding it close. If we do not have a secure sense of being able to reach for what we long for, we won't have what we need to securely hold or pull anything close. Or we might frantically reach, attempting to hold and pull close more than we can sustain—think of a dehydrated person gulping down too much water. However, when we have the safety and support we need, we can hold and pull without a distressed press on the gas. Anchored in safety, our body can flexibly use our gas pedal and brakes to navigate these movements.

You can think of these movements—yielding, pushing, reaching, and holding and pulling—as the new movements we can invite parts of us into as we explore new muscle memory. Rather than feeling stuck in the patterns of protective strategies that no longer help us, we can get curious about the kind of safety and support different parts of us might need to explore these as we move through life.

Just as I saw my niece learning to securely yield into Ally's arms, push against her at mealtime, and reach for her hand, holding and pulling her close, we can see parts of us try these new movements as they experience more and more connection and safety.

Maybe we explore sitting against a tree or lying in the grass, letting the steadiness of creation hold the full weight of our being as we yield into the present moment. And then maybe, just maybe, this starts to shift how we hold tension for the rest of the day as our body relaxes a little bit more than usual, pressing into the simplicity of being.

Maybe we see what it's like to push away from the ground as we walk or run—or we play with smacking the ground as if we're drumming—finding a way to let our body experience a sense of pushing. And then maybe, just maybe, this starts to shift how we move in the face of stressors, conflict, or relationships as our body remembers the motion and freedom of moving against or away from something.

Maybe we experiment with reaching for flowers in a garden, a snuggly stuffed animal, or a soft blanket, creating space to explore what we'd like to reach for. And then maybe, just maybe, this starts to shift how we reach for specific kinds of connection with the people we love, as our body remembers what it's like to stretch out toward what we long for.

And then maybe we play with holding the things we've reached for and pulling them close. As we let our bodies experience the subtle yet significant distinctions of these movements, we can savor the satisfaction of embracing. And maybe, just maybe, this starts to shift how we interact with loved ones, pets, or dreams that we haven't previously dared to reach for, let alone pull close and hold near.

There are relationships and environments in which each of these movements might feel easier or more difficult for us. Maybe you find yourself unable to relax and yield even when you're off the clock. Or maybe you don't reach for, hold on to, or pull close the relationships you actually want in your life. Maybe you don't push against the boss who seems to always put you down—even though deep down you want to. As we continue to get curious about the stories that have shaped the muscle memory of our movements, we can piece together what we might need to foster a sense of safety that supports exploring them in new ways.

Tapping into these ways that we move through life, along with new possibilities of movements, can feel incredibly complex. This is one reason we are moving so slowly through the ideas and exercises in each chapter. In the same way that my niece received consistent love day in and day out for months before her spirit came alive, the depths of our soul may initially seem unresponsive to our attempts to attune and extend care for them. Some parts of us may need what feels like a molasses-slow process before they feel revived. If you find yourself feeling rushed or hopeless, imagine I'm right there next to you, saying, "Every part of you can take all the time that you need to cultivate enough safety to take risks with new movements."

In the next chapter, we'll explore some of the complexities that might pop up as we try to engage with safety and these movements in new ways. Before turning there, spend a little time with the Pause & Play below.

PAUSE & PLAY:

TRACING MOVEMENTS

As we wade into these really tender spaces, I wish I could take a walk alongside you, asking you how all of this is sitting with you. I'm so curious to know if it resonates inside. I'd love to listen in on a conversation between the protective and vulnerable perspectives within you, hearing how they view the risks of being seen, known, and held—and how these risks might lead to them coming alive and moving through life in new ways.

I wonder if the idea of yielding and resting in a secure embrace brings hope for healing or feels unsafe.

I wonder if you feel permission to push against things that are not comfortable, or if you feel your needs and wants do not matter.

I wonder if the thought of reaching for connection presses on grief, reminding any part of you of love that was taken away or never known. And I wonder how this shapes the way you do or don't pull and hold things near.

I wonder if it feels possible to imagine the most hurting and hidden parts of you receiving any amount of security and care—or enough security and care that they are able to come alive and move through life in new ways.

As you reflect on your initial gut reactions to the new movements we explored in this chapter, I invite you to be curious about how you might complete the following statements:

When I imagine yielding, *simply existing without having to do anything, free to fully relax and release, the image that comes to mind is ______________________. The last time I remember feeling this way was ____.*

When I envision pushing, *being able to assert the things I do not want or need while moving them away from me, the image that comes to mind is ______________________. The last time I remember pushing against or away from something or someone was ____.*

When I picture reaching *for someone or something, expressing curiosity and taking a risk to connect with the world around me, the image that comes to mind is ______________________. The last time I remember taking the vulnerable risk to reach for someone or something was ____.*

When I think about holding *and* pulling, *bringing what I long for close to me and holding it tightly, the image that comes to mind is ______________________. The last time I remember having enough safety to know I could yield, push, reach, and ultimately hold and pull something or someone I loved close to me was*

____.

CHAPTER 10

tending to what's been wounded

It was a bright September day in East Tennessee. I was lying on a blanket in the grass, partially cooled by shade and partially warmed by the sun. A towering tree curved up toward the sky above me, creating a cozy nook to rest. I was next to a riverbank, and I watched sparkling glimmers of sunshine dance on top of the water. Sturdy bluffs hung across the river from me, like a fixed anchor of stillness alongside the moving water. I took a few breaths, and everything inside me felt as if it were melting into the ground. My body was starting to sink into yielding as I savored this idyllic moment.

Along with the lush trees and river around me, one of the main reasons I was experiencing so much bliss was because I was happily dating Elijah. As a counseling student at the time, I knew that being "in love" meant my brain and body would inevitably feel as if they were high on drugs, so I was actively trying not to let the feel-good neurotransmitters entirely distort my perspective. At the same time, I was simply happy and enjoying the pure bliss of the moment.

Then, my gut tightened. Before my internal brake system could fully slow me down into a sense of safety, my body started to press on the gas pedal. It was as if my body didn't know what to do with the peace I was feeling. Protective reactions within me weren't sure how to embrace or trust it. This was the first of several similar moments I described to my therapist Meredith, prompting her to say, "Your body doesn't know that you're safe." The confusing thing to me was that, in that moment and that season of life, I absolutely was.

Looking for the Coming Storm

Because our bodies are wired to help us survive, they remember experiences of pain and loss and try to help us avoid similar threats in the future.[1] As I lay in the grass that day, this was exactly what was starting to stir inside of me—a part of me was concerned that this sense of safety wasn't *actually* dependable.

In a previous relationship, I had tasted a sense of safety—early on my brain and body had been high on feel-good neurotransmitters as well. I thought I could trust the other person so that even when the "newly in love" phase wore off, we'd experience a shared and sweet fondness throughout our lives together. And then we didn't.

Instead of a happily-ever-after, I was lied to, cheated, and mistreated by someone I deeply trusted. Instead of my brain and body resting in safety through connection with another person, my worst nightmares darkened the light of security. Through that experience, the vulnerability of safety became fused with a lack of safety. The depths of my soul learned that people aren't actually safe and can't be fully trusted. The world was no longer a safe-enough place for me to yield in, especially when it came to romantic relationships.

It didn't matter that my thinking brain could logically prove me wrong: Of course there were some safe people out there somewhere who could be trusted. This just didn't matter to the depths of my soul—the core of me—that held a visceral fear I could not reason with. How could I ever again let myself sink into a vulnerable state of safety, especially relationally? Protective perspectives within me saw this as too large of a risk—yielding into safety could leave me too vulnerable. More than this, reaching for—or trying to hold and pull—someone close exposed me to the potential pain of loss or harm. And from that protective perspective, parts of me had already put together a plan of how to guard myself from this kind of vulnerability.

Prior to dating Elijah, I was in grad school and had pretty much resolved that my safest life plan would be to complete my two degrees, move to Europe, adopt some cats, and call it a day. You might think I'm joking, but I actually voiced these words at the time, fully intending to follow through with them. I simply didn't think I would find anyone with a tender-enough heart for me to feel sufficiently safe and take the risk of being in a relationship again. Europe had been home in my childhood and felt safe, as did fluffy and snuggly cats.

This plan certainly felt safer than putting myself in the vulnerable spot of trusting another person again. I wasn't sure I could survive being deeply hurt a second time by someone who had vowed to love me for the rest of our lives. And so, in my Europe-cat plan, I was trying to secure the perfect conditions to be able to yield, push, reach, hold, and pull—conditions dictated by a protective perspective that ironically wouldn't let me relax enough to even yield, the first of these movements.

And then, just when I thought my Europe-cat plan was secure, I met Elijah. He was brilliant, kind, strong, empathic, and ruggedly beautiful. No amount of logic in my thinking brain could shield me from the slew of feel-good neurotransmitters that made my heart swoon after we met. We were friends and classmates in grad school, bonding over our love of ancient languages and losing ourselves in our deep thoughts and feelings. On that September day in East Tennessee, I was in town with him to meet his family.

Despite sitting in the sunshine under clear skies, I was looking around for the coming storm. My protective perspective infused me with hypervigilance, watching to assess any risk to the vulnerable depths inside that still carried wounds that had nearly flattened them. The story these parts had learned was that people can say they will honor you, be faithful to you, and care for you—they might even seem to do so for a while—before inflicting devastating pain without concern for how it might harm you or others.

And so, in the present, my body was remembering the past. As Meredith could clearly see, my body didn't know I was safe. I knew that things appeared safe relationally, but that is how they had seemed in my prior relationship. Back then this sense of safety had been linked with jarring heartache. As you may have heard, neurons that fire together wire together.[2] My brain and body didn't yet know that it would be possible to detangle what had been wired together so that I could experience a sense of safety *without* the jarring heartache that had been mixed up with it.

The ways that a sense of safety can be confusingly fused with pain, grief, or fear often makes exploring new movements feel unsafe at the gut level of our autonomic nervous system, even when they are indeed secure. This can be frustrating and disorienting for our body, as well as the parts we carry within. Rather than trying to force immediate relief or rest that may still be inaccessible to certain facets of ourselves, we can get curious about what makes clinging to our old muscle memory feel more comfortable than exploring new movements.

PAUSE & PLAY:

YIELDING INTO SAFETY

I invite you to be curious about how your past experiences with safety, or lack of safety, have shaped how your body yields into or moves away from it.

See what it's like to give voice to the parts of you that are driving the car in these movements:

My body is able to yield and relax most when ________________.
When this happens, I know my body is gently pressing on the brakes because ________________________________.

Even when I'm resting or on vacation, the ways I still feel tension or hypervigilance include ________________________.
When this happens, I know my body is pressing on the gas pedal because ________________________________.

Even if I have space to rest or am on vacation, the ways I feel my body slam the brakes and shut down (going numb, feeling disoriented, or disconnecting) rather than restfully sink into safety, include ____________________. When this happens, I know my body is slamming on the brakes instead of restfully pressing on the brakes because ____________________________________.

After exploring the questions above, see what pops up in your thoughts, emotions, body sensations, and memories as you read the following prompt:

If protective perspectives within me wrote a thesis statement about why the world isn't a safe place, they would say ____.

In addition to getting curious about what you notice right now, consider planning a time this week when you could sit down and give yourself space to write a lengthier response from the viewpoint of protective perspectives within.

Safety Is Not Always Simple

Not long ago, a hawk flew directly in front of my windshield while I was driving seventy-five miles an hour on a highway. The bird immediately shattered my windshield, which thankfully had been designed not to collapse. Remarkably, there was no collision after the impact. A friend was riding in the car with me, and we both sat there a bit stunned afterward, trying to understand what had just happened. Neither of us had ever had a bird fly into our car, let alone one whose wingspan covered a large windshield.

While my thinking brain wasn't sure how to sort out what happened, the way my body experienced driving shifted. For the next couple of months, whenever a bird flew anywhere near my car, I felt my gut tighten and my breathing become shallow. It was as if my body was bracing for another large bird to hit my windshield. Even if a bird with a three-inch wingspan flew near my vehicle, my body would tense. I told the friend who was with me when the bird hit us what I had been noticing, and she immediately told me she had been observing the same reactions inside herself.

This is a small example of how neuroception gets tangled up in a web of body memories from past experiences. After they are flooded with a sense of danger or panic, it's reasonable that our body might decide for us that the world's not a safe place—especially when anything in the present reminds us of danger or panic in the past. It's reasonable that my brain and body no longer feel confident that birds will not collide with my car. Now that I have a concrete experience of it happening, I know it is possible for birds, even large ones, to fly directly into my windshield, threatening the safety of anyone in my car or other vehicles around me.

If that is a reasonable reaction to a small incident, how much more compassion do our bodies need for how they hold the wounds of deeply engrained experiences? The ways we are wired and the experiences we have walked through shape our neuroception—how our brains and bodies perceive and experience safety or lack of safety. This neuroception then informs whether protective reactions will allow space to yield, sinking into safety and flexible movements, or will move us into protective strategies. This can become tricky because, while it's a good design, it's based on our perception, which doesn't always match what's happening around us.

This is why exploring the stories our body knows can be so helpful. When we get curious, we can trace strands of stories that still live in and through us today, helping us understanding why yielding into safety is not always simple.

Before we begin learning practices to help restore safety to our systems, I want to pause and honor that it's completely normal for safety to feel complex, especially when we've lived through certain life circumstances. We may have had an unpredictable caregiver who could be kind and present one moment and distant or harsh the next. We may have lost a significant attachment figure or been harmed or neglected by someone who was supposed to keep us safe. Unfortunately, most of us have experienced some form of one of these losses, making safety a tricky thing to trust.

As we explore cultivating safety for parts of us that distrust it, please hear me—you are not alone if this feels complex, confusing, foreign, or unsafe. Imagine for a moment that I'm right next to you, gently reminding each and every part of you that there is nothing wrong with you if you don't currently resonate with any of these words or practices—and it's okay if this book on its own does not enable you to connect with and trust safety. As we consider how parts of you might start to trust in or restore a felt sense of security, it's okay if you need to move so slowly that, from the outside, it seems that there's no movement at all.

This is some of the most raw and sacred work we can open ourselves up to. Find your pace and the people you need to walk the road with you. Remember: It's okay to be right where you are. It's okay to take a break. It's okay to ask for help.

What Does Safety Feel Like?

While I was writing the first draft of this chapter in my office, one of my cats was stretched out on the floor beside me, blissfully basking in the warmth of the sun streaming through the window. This not-so-little guy was once the runt of the litter we fostered, one of two cats that we adopted. As he grew, he pressed hard into his name, Sleepy, taking twice as many naps as his sister Happy each day. And when Sleepy rests like this, he's unconcerned with any potential strangers coming to the door or birds chirping in the front yard. When his body determines he is safe, he is not hypervigilant or provoked to fight. Instead, he gets to simply *be*, which often includes purring, nuzzling, and even drooling.

As I looked over at him, his breathing was slow and his body had fully melted into the ground, a most perfect depiction of yielding. Rather than melting as though he was falling apart, he melted in a way that left him fully intact, sturdy and anchored in the carpet beneath him. As I reached down to scratch his chin, his eyes remained closed tight as he nestled into his nap, knowing that he could rest safely alongside me. He recognized my touch and knew this routine, where he serves as my honorary co-writer and co-therapist in my home office. Few things could disturb him as he securely rested alongside me. His body knew he was safe.

If he were in another setting, or if our setting was invaded by another human or animal that he does not associate with security and rest, he would shift states immediately, moving into protective strategies. The very moment he would hear, smell, or sense an unknown human or animal, he would bolt and flee, pull his claws out to fight, get low to the ground to fawn in submission, find me to hide behind, or if he were terrified, possibly freeze or flop on the ground. Each of these responses is just a millisecond away if external or internal cues inform his neuroception that things are no longer peacefully safe.

His sister Happy requires more specific conditions to yield. Even though both of them were raised by me from the time they were five weeks old, their dispositions are different. Happy is quick to push away from us when we reach for her, living up to classic cat stereotypes. She has to be the one to reach for us. She needs the house to be quiet and still before she'll even consider coming close. And if someone else is in or near the house, she hides. In the sweetest of still moments when no one else is around, if she wants to connect and chooses to initiate contact, she doesn't just reach for us nonchalantly. With the calm of the quiet and known humans around her, she will hold and pull our hands close to snuggle with her, filling the silent house with her purrs.

Similarly, the conditions we need to enter a state of safety vary between people. And like these sweet animals, it's only when we feel safe that we can connect with the present moment and others most deeply. When we feel safe, our bodies let our defenses down, and we are able to yield, breathing more deeply than we would if activated to move through some sort of stress or threat. Anchored in safety, a protective perspective is not cued to move in the muscle memory of protective strategies, and vulnerable depths of us have more breathing space. This is the place where we most flexibly have access to all parts that make up the whole of us, and where other people will likely see the most open, authentic, and playful versions of us.

Depending on our muscle memory, safety can feel refreshing—or it can feel threatening, like we are exposing a wound to harm. If we fly through most of our days with a rush of adrenaline coursing through our veins, the experience of simply being will likely feel disorienting. If we chronically oscillate between stress and shutdown states or find ourselves often stuck in the rut of being immobilized in overwhelm, then being present and engaged with the world around us in a state of safety will probably feel strange. If hurting parts of us have experienced painful wounds when we thought we were safe, then the vulnerability of safety will reasonably feel like a danger zone.

In whatever ways feeling exposed in safety might be complicated for us, it's important to remember that vulnerability in and of itself does not inherently indicate weakness. When we open ourselves in safety, we inhabit a beautiful state that's anchored deeply in our body, rather than tensely reacting in stress or shutting down in overwhelm. And that openness is crucial to building relationships and connecting with others in an authentic and healthy way.

Now if our bodies were relaxed and open to the world because we thought we were safe but then something happened—something that was *not* safe—a protective perspective might form within, deciding that in order to guard vulnerable depths of us from harm, we must keep them on lockdown. And while our thinking brain might be in on this conversation, often these protective strategies are embedded in muscle memory at the level of our autonomic nervous systems. Often this means our thinking brain is never even consulted on how open we want to be in our relationships.

This doesn't mean that when we don't trust someone or something, we are engaged in self-sabotage or have become our own enemy. It actually means we're responding reasonably to what we have experienced in life. Pause and reread that last sentence again with a deep breath and a hand over your heart. You might even embrace your body as you read it.

Maybe you resonate with a part of you that seems to ruin relationships, unsure of why certain circumstances seem to be a cue to run away and flee from intimacy rather than yielding into a sense of rest. Or maybe you feel like the part of you that self-sabotages your relationships responds to any cue by starting a fight, ultimately pushing away your chance for safety and connection.

Maybe you hate yourself for never asserting what you really think or feel, fawning with others to try to keep the peace, sick and tired of never experiencing peace because no one really knows you or what you'd like to reach for, hold, and pull close to you.

Or maybe you scapegoat a part of you that seems to find or reach for connection in unhelpful spaces, seemingly complicating your life rather than enriching it with the intimacy you long for.

Maybe relational conflict causes something inside you to freeze, collapse (flop), or disconnect (fragment) from the present moment. Maybe it feels as if there's a wall you can't get over, one that keeps you from reaching for the person or people you most want to find and be with.

If any of these scenarios rings true in our body and bones, I wonder: What is the story that shaped these movements, and how did safety get complicated in that narrative? In what ways might a lack of safety have been fused with safety? What if we learned to trace the complexities of these fusions so we could see the compassion and care that parts of us might need before they can risk yielding into safety in new ways? And then, what if we responded with that compassion and care, working *with* these parts of us to create new narratives and new movements that anchor us in the present rather than feeling trapped in the past?

PAUSE & PLAY:

RESTORING SAFETY

You've been investing in restoring safety in every Pause & Play we've walked through together. The simple act of slowing down, connecting with and listening to your body, and getting in touch with different parts beneath the surface are all ways we can anchor ourselves in the present moment. Along with this, noticing what does and does not feel comfortable—what prompts stress or shutdown inside of us—gives us clues about what safety does and does not feel like in our body.

Before jumping to try to force or establish safety within, let's sit with the movements that might feel like they're working against us. Simply *being with* what happens inside is one of the most powerful ways to cultivate or restore safety.

> In what ways does your body tense up or disconnect around spaces of potential safety?
>
> In what ways do you sense that your body would prefer to press on the gas pedal or slam on the brakes rather than yielding into safety?

See what it's like to act out how these movements feel internally. Even if it feels silly, use your whole body—arms, legs, fingers, toes, head, torso, and more—to express how your internal gas pedal or brake system moves your body away from yielding into safety. Embodying these movements can help translate something that feels elusive into something that is tangibly known.

With another deep breath, scan your body to notice how you might feel open to your internal brake system lulling you into a new or restored sense of safety.

If this does not yet seem like it's in the realm of possibility, see what it's like to act out what it might hypothetically look like if a person's internal brake system were to lull their body into a sense of safety. Again, use your whole body—arms, legs, fingers, toes, head, torso, and more—to play out what you envision this might look like. Embodying these movements can help translate something that feels elusive into something that is tangibly known.

CHAPTER 11

tending to hidden longings

Anytime I see my oldest sister and her kids, I know to brace for four loud and chaotic conversations happening all at once. In a moment's time, her daughter and three younger sons will flock to me in excitement, pummeling me with stories and hugs before I know what's happened. It's as though each of them is going to burst if they don't get out the very thing they so desperately want to tell me in that moment. I can tell from their little voices that they know they're all vying for my attention. Each gets louder in hopes of being the one heard above the others.

One of my nephews will grab my arm, looking up at me as he tells a thrilling story about something that happened in a favorite movie. Through the chaotic movements of his entire body, he shows me what happened in a fight scene. With no breaths in between, he tells me, "And *then*, the one guy went like *this*, and *then* the other guys went like *that*" as he moves his body in concert with his sound effects. He's bringing me into the movie scene with him, a film he wishes we could have snuggled up and watched together. His reenactments tell me, *I wish you were there with me. I like it when we're together. Sharing this with you is different from experiencing it without you.*

Simultaneously, another nephew holds my left hand, looking up at me with a sad gaze as he's wading in the grief of a disappointing day. His big brown eyes lock with mine, asking me, *Will you join me in my sadness? Will you be with me for this moment?* And then, as he hangs his head down, he says in a low voice, "Can I tell you something that happened?" His shoulders droop forward as his body carries the vulnerability of his story, almost like he's debating whether to curl into himself or invite me into his sadness. He reaches out his finger to show me an injury, explaining with precision exactly how he got hurt and what it felt like. The somber pain in his eyes asks me, *Do you care? If I pull you in to be with me, will you come feel this with me?*

At the same time, a third nephew skips up to me and places a stuffed animal in front of my face, reaching his arm up as high as he can to try to reach my eye level with his plushy creature. As he waves it around he shouts, "*This* is my *axolotl!* I saw one at school *in real life! They are real!* But this one isn't real. It's just a stuffed animal." He bops his head side to side as he continues reciting facts he's learned about these silly little salamanders. Then he pauses to ask, "Have you ever seen an axolotl in real life?" His excitement and curiosity invite me to skip with him. He's asking me, *Do you care about the things I care about? Are my joy and excitement meaningful to you? Will you learn about the world with me?*

All the while, my teenage niece walks alongside us, towering over her younger brothers. She smiles with anxious excitement, ready to talk about her friends and the many books she's been reading. Without skipping a beat, she jumps right into a story: "So on the way to school the other day, my friend Corinne, who rides the same bus as me . . ." She continues on, pacing her speech with her steps, unconcerned by the competition of her brothers, happy to be less outnumbered by boys as I'm next to her. As she tells me about her life, her sweet smile and story ask, *Does the mundane of my life matter to you? Will you keep listening if I share more?*

Each of these conversations invites me into a unique rhythm and pace. And if I enter in to *be with* my niece and nephews in these moments, I will start to move with the cadences of what's happening inside each of them. As their internal gas pedals speed up and their speech and movements accelerate, my internal gas pedal also feels pressed if I am tracking with them. I can feel the urgency, excitement, or fear that they're not only telling me about but that they're also asking me to witness and be with in that moment.

If the internal brake systems inside them slow things down, my internal brake system is likely to do so as well, as if we're going from a 55 mile-per-hour speed zone to a 25 mile-per-hour school zone. I can feel the heaviness and thickness of the emotion they're feeling and inviting me to feel with them. Sometimes it even feels like we're pulling over to the side of the road, needing a minute to pause before hitting the gas again. As my nervous system goes along for the ride with each of theirs, different parts of me inside feel conflicted—I'm being asked to drive different roads with different speeds, all at the same time!

Internally I'm torn as one nephew wants me to join with him and get as loud as we can in excitement about a new movie. We're stepping on the gas in a way that is fun, connected, and safe. At the same time, though, another nephew is asking me to pump the brakes and slow down with him in a somber moment of connection. I want to be with both of them right where they are, matching how they're moving through the moment they're inviting me to share.

But no matter how hard I try, I cannot change the math of the problem in front of me. I can't fully track with and mirror all four of their paces and rhythms at once. With only one face and a single presence to offer, I initially swirl in the chaos before kindly reminding them that there's only one of me and four of them, and we'll have to take things one at a time. There's just no way for me to lock eyes and be present with each of them, entering into the stories and moments they are reaching out to share with me.

The different ways these little ones move through their emotions are external pictures of what happens inside us when distinct parts of us reach for attunement. One part of us might be stressed or excited, pressing on the gas, while another part of us feels overwhelmed or tired, hitting the brakes. Sometimes it even feels like a part of us has put a concrete cinder block on the gas or the brakes, trying to demand that we stay in stress or shutdown, making it feel nearly impossible to get out of our current state. These nuances can flood our entire system, making us feel confused and even disoriented as we try to tune in with everything that's happening inside.

After a long week, you might find yourself trying to negotiate between a part of you that excitedly wants to enjoy your free time with a favorite hobby, an exhausted part of you that just carried your workweek, and an inner critic who is reminding you of all the chores around the house that you'll probably fail to complete.

Both protective perspectives and vulnerable depths of us will need different kinds of patience as we tend within. It might take time for protective viewpoints to trust that we are on the same team—that we both want what's best for our well-being—even if we sometimes have different ideas about what that looks like. Like soldiers who have faithfully defended a post for years, parts of us that take on a protective perspective might not immediately believe that we know how to look after what they've been guarding.

Tender and vulnerable depths of us might need time to trust that there is enough safety for them to come out of hiding. Like scared and wounded animals, they may find it too risky to respond to a helping hand. Sometimes from these perspectives we can't even imagine being seen or heard, let alone cared for. When we're used to *not* having what we need, it will often feel more comfortable and predictable to continue going without.

And intermixed with it all, we might have inner critics who judge and shame our efforts, seemingly refusing to work together, tearing us down every step of the way. Like seemingly hostile cats who won't stop hissing and scratching, these parts of us sometimes require the most time to learn to trust, sometimes requiring more patience than we feel we have to offer.

PAUSE & PLAY:

HERDING CATS

Real talk for a moment here: Tending to the depths of the soul can feel like herding cats—and not a cute scenario where a cat lover is caring for a new litter of adorable kittens but a not-so-adorable situation in which someone who doesn't like cats is trying to corral them, only to feel overwhelmed and frustrated by these sneaky little panthers. . . .

If you are feeling good about tending to the depths of your soul, great! If you are feeling overwhelmed or apprehensive, let's pause for a moment and create space to consider the ways this work can feel like it's more than we can manage. Feel free to shake out your arms and legs with a deep breath before reflecting on the questions below.

When I think about tending to all the depths of my soul, the imagery that comes to mind is:

- ☐ Herding cats I can't get under control.
- ☐ Screaming children I don't know what to do with.
- ☐ A room full of withering plants that need care I don't know how to provide.
- ☐ Other: ______________________________________

When I think about how I would like to imagine tending to the depths of my soul, I envision: ______________________________ .
(Fill in the blank with what pops up internally.)

I invite you to explore the shifts you would love to see in the way you imagine tending to the depths of your soul, particularly the parts of you that you are used to being disconnected from, maybe don't like, or are unsure what to do with.

How would you like to interact with the depths of your soul?

What kind of relational dynamics do you hope to develop with different parts of yourself?

When some people imagine entrusting some of the care their parts need into God's hands, they feel like a large load has been taken off their shoulders. For others, this thought creates anxiety or discomfort because it doesn't feel safe. As we begin to work with any wary parts of us, we never want to force them into spiritual platitudes or to create new muscle memory that includes spiritual bypassing.

Rather than shaming any parts of yourself for not feeling like they can or want to yield into God's care, simply notice your internal reaction when you think about this possibility, using the following reflection prompt.

When I think about entrusting some of the care of these parts of me into God's hands, my initial reaction is to feel:

- ☐ tense
- ☐ like I can take a deeper breath
- ☐ anxiety in my gut
- ☐ my body relax

If any parts of you don't feel comfortable inviting God to care for them, rather than shaming yourself, consider the following as an option for how you might embody God's patience, kindness, and compassion. Ask yourself:

If I had a friend who answered these questions as I did, how would I respond to them?

Would I respond with shame?

Would I respond with understanding?

What would it be like if I were to offer myself the same kind of kindness I might offer to someone else?

Being Present

If I feel stretched when outnumbered four to one with my oldest sister's kids, I feel overextended when my whole family is together and my nieces and nephews outnumber me six to one. I'm fully aware that I can't attune with each of them in every moment in the ways I wish I could. To really be with each of them is an equation without an easy solution—there is only one of me, so we have to find a rhythm that works for everyone.

And let me tell you, these little ones can tell if I'm really listening to them. They are aware when I'm looking back at them or looking at something else. When I lock my eyes with theirs without being distracted by anything around me, they know I'm really listening and fully *there*. If I'm on my phone, trying to complete some other task, or toggling between multiple nieces and nephews, they can tell they're getting only strands of me, not all of me. It's not just my physical presence that tells them I'm with them. It's when they can see my face attuned with theirs that they securely know that all of me is present with them.

This is because our presence is intricately connected with our face. Think for a moment about all the little facial muscles that communicate emotions and connection that others can't see unless our face is, well, facing them! In the simplest way, our presence is directed wherever our face is directed. We are uniquely able to give attention to what we see right in front of us. We can reach for what's right in front of us and be reached for by those who are right in front of us. The people and things we can slow down with, tune in with, and tend toward require proximity and presence.

Going back to the ancient voices in the Psalms, we see these were people who understood the significance of face-to-face attunement. Even though they didn't use clinical jargon to describe it, they knew what neuroscience teaches us today—being face-to-face with another creates connection.[1]

The psalmists cry out, "Do not hide your face from me!" over and over,[2] reaching out for God's face to be near.[3] In their pleas, they aren't asking for an intellectual idea of God. They are looking to pull a personal presence close, a presence they also ask to hear them.[4] It's clear they know that God being *with them* is not an idea to hold in their thinking brains. They show us that God's presence is not just a platitude, but a face.

I love the treasures we can find behind our translations of these ancient words. In Hebrew, the word that we translate as *face* is the same word that we translate as *presence*. We see this word rendered a number of ways across the book of Exodus, a book that is all about how God saw the pain and affliction of the enslaved children of Israel and responded to liberate them. Whenever we read about God's presence being with or going before the people, the Hebrew could also be literally translated as God's face being with or going before them.

A Hebrew professor I studied with suggested we consider *face-presence* as a helpful translation of this word in the context of Exodus.[5] I love how bringing the words *face* and *presence* together communicates the tender spaces where God is relationally *with* the children of Israel. I also love reflecting on how the wording *face-presence* highlights that when we offer our face to another, we are offering our presence.

Being Seen

It used to be accepted by many that "children should be seen and not heard." Following this train of thought, no one was concerned with how adults might attune with a child. Instead, the child's behavior—not their need for engagement with attachment figures—was the priority. Sometimes without realizing it, we can adopt this same mindset toward parts of ourselves, making it seem unreasonable that they are crying out, needing more of our presence. We might label these parts as needy or dramatic and in turn dismiss their longings and cries. It might take a long time for all parts of us to be sold on the idea that it is worth tuning in with every strand of our being.

We might also feel like we have no idea what it looks like to attune with what's happening within, especially if we haven't received attunement from others. The good news here is that when we simply slow down with what's happening inside, we are actually already exploring the movement of attunement.

Say we're walking into the grocery store or reading this book when we start to notice stress stirring beneath the surface. We can try out attunement by simply slowing down and observing what's happening, getting curious about which parts of us are driving the car and why they might be pressing on the gas in that moment. Even if we don't have exact clarity, we can simply pause, breathe, and notice something like, *All right, someone in me is pressing the gas. I'm feeling anxiety in my gut and tightness in my chest. That's interesting. I wonder what prompted that movement inside.* We might not know why we're feeling anxiety, but the anxious parts of us inside can be witnessed—seen and heard—as we slow down to acknowledge what's happening within. And as we continue to slow down and listen in, we might receive feedback that tells us what an anxious part of us most needs in that moment or the week ahead.

Or maybe as you try to do these Pause & Play exercises, you feel as if there's a massive brick wall that keeps you from connecting with what's happening inside. Rather than having an answer or solution, you might simply attune with what's *not* stirring within. You might just notice what's happening in that moment, reflecting, *Hmm, I feel like I'm hitting a wall, like the brakes are overriding anything I'm trying to do. I feel numb and disconnected—and frustrated that I feel numb and disconnected. I want to get this right but I can't even figure out how to start.* This kind of reflection alone offers a sense of presence that lets parts of us know that they are now seen and heard, and that we accept them as they are rather than expect them to immediately get their act together.

When we pay attention to what's happening internally, we may notice that parts of us long for connection and responses that feel like too much for us to hold on our own. Maybe we feel disappointed after a friend cancels plans, and slowing down makes us realize, *Oh wow, someone inside is crying—like full-on ugly crying inconsolably! I don't want to feel this. This feels like way too much for me to try to care for on my own. It just reinforces how alone I already feel.*

So, what do we do when tending to what's happening within simply feels like too much? Rather than reinforcing old messages that we are too much or we need to cut off emotions, I'd love to share with you one way that spiritual integration with parts work has been formative in my life. When we view the longings that stir inside of us as sacred spaces we might invite God into, we can explore how this might breathe life into spaces that feel like death.

As we invite God to join us in tending to the depths of our souls, we can see what it's like to imagine God attuning with us, carrying what feels too heavy for us to carry alone. We might envision this in a specific kind of imagery that paints a picture of peace internally. Or maybe we experience this in the tangible interactions with another person who's embodying God's love and care. Some of us might prefer to write, draw, or create some sort of depiction of what we've been carrying, seeing a physical representation of what we're looking to unburden.

If any of these examples of spiritual integration don't feel safe right now, please remember you have full permission to choose how you move though these paragraphs, and you are of course free to move ahead to the next chapter. If you want to continue walking with me through the words below, we're going to survey the raw vulnerability of where we are presently—the raw vulnerability of the landscape of our souls.

Whatever your starting point, please know that my words are not prescriptions about how you should tend to parts of yourself with spiritual integration. Instead, my words are simply an invitation to explore where you are and whether you might long for things to be different. It's okay to be right where you are, not jumping to how you think you should interact with God's presence.

I'm curious: How does the thought of God's face-presence being with us—especially the most hidden or wounded parts—sit with you? And rather than looking for the right answer, I'm curious: What's the most honest answer? Rather than jumping to how we think we should react or respond here, let's slow down and sit with what's happening inside.

Maybe the idea of God holding the most overwhelmed parts of you brings relief. Maybe it brings panic.

Maybe the idea of God's hands holding things together, including all parts of you, feels like the secure anchor you long for. Maybe it feels restrictive or controlling.

Maybe the idea of the divine living in you makes you feel hopeful, like there's a blossoming garden in your soul that has all the nourishment that every part of you needs. Maybe it feels impossible or uncomfortable.

Maybe the idea of God embodied in the love and kindness of a caregiver, real or imagined, brings a sense of peace and trust. Maybe the idea of any kind of caregiver brings unease or painful memories.

Wherever you are, wherever each part of you is, I invite you to be curious about how spirituality might be more deeply woven into this whole process of slowing down, tuning in with your body, and tending toward the depths of your soul. In any ways you feel you can be curious about this, slowly read through the statements below, noticing the feedback from your body as you read each one. Remember, you can pause and utilize the grounding prompts on pages 24–25 at any time.

Taking a deep breath, contemplate how the Spirit might breathe life into you as you explore new ways of flexibly moving in concert with your internal gas pedal and brake system. How might this breath reach and fill the corners of your soul where parts of you have been hidden or neglected?

Placing your hands on your body, consider how Immanuel—God with us—felt and demonstrated deep compassion. How might Christ be with you as you tune in and tend toward what stirs within your body?

And how might the steadfast presence of God as a parent, who is with you in every breath, bring restorative peace or comfort?

Again, we're not seeking right or wrong answers here, we're simply being curious and honest about what's stirring inside. If you notice parts of you pushing against any of these questions, I invite you to be with these parts just as they are. You might ask one or more of them if they might share a story with you to help you understand what's happening inside or what they need to feel safe. You can consider the ways they may not have received this kind of care before and feel uncertain that they will ever receive grace or kindness, especially as it relates to God.

When we reflect on questions like these, we can explore the ways that our spirituality is intertwined with all the facets of our embodied being.

We can also consider how bringing all parts of us into our spirituality might help us heal and flourish in new ways. Just as spiritual trauma, harm, and abuse have a profound and holistic impact, tending to all of the strands of our being, including spiritually, can cultivate a profound and holistic healing.

If any parts of us don't see God near us, or don't experience God's presence as comforting, ignoring this or trying to will it to be different is unlikely to feel helpful. To tend to these spaces, we need to know their honest starting point, which I invite you to explore in the prompts below.

PAUSE & PLAY:

WHERE DO I SEE GOD?

Find items inside or outside your house that could represent different parts of you. You might pick up rocks, sticks, leaves, stuffed animals, dolls, fruits or vegetables—truly anything. Then select an item, or items, to represent God. As you gather these objects, place them on the ground or on a table, exploring how together they depict the state of your soul.[6]

Rather than trying to set up a scene that would mimic a Sunday school flannel board, create an honest and raw depiction of how these parts of you view God. You might have parts of you that see God as angry or harsh, while other parts of you see God as kind and loving. You might view the three persons of the Trinity differently as well. Consider gathering objects for these different depictions, remembering this exercise is not about creating a theologically accurate representation of God, but instead, an honest expression of what's happening inside—something that is certainly no mystery to God.

Once you have gathered objects that represent parts of you along with how parts of you view God, read over the following questions to see if they help you place each one.

> Are there any parts of you that feel that God is far away or distant?
> If so, where would you like to place the objects that represent
> these parts in relation to the objects that represent God?

Are there any parts of you that want to be hidden from God? If so, where would you like to place the objects that represent these parts in relation to the objects that represent God?

Are there any parts of you that feel that God is near? If so, where would you like to place the objects that represent these parts in relation to the objects that represent God?

Are there any parts of you that don't see God anywhere? If so, where would you like to place the objects that represent these parts in relation to the objects that represent God?

Are there any parts of you that want to be protected from the idea of God being near? If so, where would you like to place the objects that represent these parts in relation to the objects that represent God?

Are there any parts of you that want barriers to be broken so they can sense God's nearness? If so, where would you like to place the objects that represent these parts in relation to the objects that represent God?

As you play with this depiction of the state of your soul, consider the following nuances as well:

Which direction are different parts of me facing?

Which direction do I have God facing?

Do I need to add any other objects or items to express anything else that is stirring inside?

After you have spent time with this depiction of what's happening within, consider the ways you long for your internal world to look. Ask yourself:

Do I long for the relationships here to look different? If so, how?

Do I want to move any of these objects to play with how these dynamics might look different? If so, how would I move them?

If I move them, how does it feel to see the picture in front of me shift? What happens internally as I play with this visual externally?

Before moving on, consider how you'd like to honor and close your time with these objects and what they represent. Ask yourself:

Would I like to take a picture of this to remember how this looked before putting things away?

Would I like to leave these objects out on a table or in a place where I can see them daily?

Would I like to move these objects so they represent some sort of hope, resolve, or redemption that would be significant for any parts of me to see?

CHAPTER 12

tending to new movements

"As we walk, I will follow your pace," I told my client Jess at the beginning of our first walk-and-talk session. I had recently completed training in outdoor therapy models and was now introducing her to the unique elements of this kind of therapy. Until now, our sessions had been held in my office, where we sat across from each other, anchored by the trees outside the window, the coolness of the kinetic sand we'd dig our hands into, and the soothing sound of water cascading down a small waterfall on the shelf beside us.

I assured Jess that I would follow her lead on our walk, assuming I'd have no issues keeping up with her, even if she was a fast walker. I absolutely love walking and hiking, and was bursting with joy at seeing my dream of providing this form of therapy become reality. It wouldn't be long, though, before I remembered my father's lifelong cautions about what happens when you assume things.

When we set off, our bodies were anchored by the strike of our heels against the earth, the gentle flow of the river beside us, and the swaying trees that we could reach out and touch. I delicately held a new tension inside, wondering what it might look like to attune with her now that we were side by side and continually moving, rather than face-to-face and sitting still. An anxious part of me started to worry, thinking, *Oh no—what will this be like for her since I can't offer her as much eye contact? Does it feel like I'm disconnected? I have to look down or I'll trip on these tree roots, and my neck can't stay turned that long without hurting . . .*

My thoughts were abruptly interrupted as my leg muscles locked up and my calves started to burn. We were continuously moving much more quickly than I had anticipated or stretched for. As my father's words rang in my ears, I regretted my assumption that I'd have no issues keeping up with any walking pace a client might set.

Before I could finish wondering, *How in the world is she maintaining such a fast pace?*, my internal dialogue was stopped in its tracks. I realized that the living and breathing embodiment of anxiety and stress that Jess wanted to address in therapy—the very thing she felt she was working against—was playing out right in front of me.

After describing yet another night of little sleep, Jess threw her hands in front of her, gesturing her confusion and frustration. "I know that I can prepare for work presentations ahead of time. I don't need to stay up the night before, panicking, which leaves me in worse shape for the actual meeting. If I know this, why do I keep doing it?"

And then somehow, in a way that defied the laws of physics, Jess picked up the pace even more. Cue my father's words again, and cue more burning in my calves.

As my legs scampered to keep up with hers, I turned my head to meet her eyes for a moment. I placed a hand over my heart and another over my abdomen and asked, "What's happening inside right now?"

More than anything around us, this question was the anchor during our times together. This was a question I had asked before, and one she knew I would continue to ask again and again.

Jess was aware that I wasn't suggesting she *stop it* or *get it together*. She also knew I was not telling her she should utilize some sort of behavior modification tactic. She understood I was inviting her to slow down and tune in with what was happening inside—to slow down and *be with* what was happening there.

She didn't need to find words to express what was stirring within—her body was already showing me. As she ferociously charged ahead, she was not simply describing the anxiety and stress she felt in her body. Instead, she was being moved by that anxiety and stress. It was as though I was hearing them speak in a new way, listening to an internal voice that propelled us forward at a speed I believe has only ever been used by professional speed walkers.

As our fast pace was fueled by her internal gas pedal and she had freedom to push us forward, there was space for her to speak from a place inside that I had not yet heard from. And as she moved through this space in a new way, I witnessed Jess start to move *with* the anxiety and stress that she felt had been driving her crazy, rather than simply being moved by it. It wasn't long before I realized I was not the only one witnessing what was speaking inside her.

She named the living and breathing panic in her gut that would keep her up the night before presentations, churning with fear that she might lose her job if she made a mistake. She detailed the worries of a younger her who didn't know if there would be food on the table because, back then, every day of work was critical to her very survival. She could notice the muscle memory that fueled her to fight through her workdays, stuck in a gear of stress. And she voiced her longing to find a way out of the feedback loop that she could see was no longer helping her.

After a few more steps, she reflected on the complexities of the conflict she was carrying inside, saying, "I think I forget that I have a good and steady job now, and that my bosses actually like me. Even if I do totally mess up a presentation, I know I'm not going to get fired. But I guess there's a younger part of me that's stuck *back there*, back in the days when I had no sense of job security or security anywhere in my life."

Her words still carried frustration with a hint of *Why can't you just get it together* directed toward this younger version of her. Her body forged ahead as her head shook in confusion.

I turned toward her and gently said, "I wonder what eighteen-year-old you might need in order to know that she's going to be okay—to know that *you* are going to be okay."

While continuing to put one foot in front of the other, Jess quickly rattled off, "I mean, everything I just said. I have a good job now that I'm established in. My life is stable enough that even if something crazy happened and I did lose my job, I would be okay. Things are so different now from back then." Her shoulders shrugged, seeming to say, *I already know these things. What difference will it make to think about them again?*

I looked back at her, seeing the defeat stretched across her face. After a short pause, I said, "I wonder what it might be like to let this younger you know that you're forty-seven and to tell her all the ways your job and your life look different after the last twenty-nine years. Almost like bringing her into the present with you, and showing her what life is like here. Can you imagine letting her know she's safe and no longer has to carry that anxiety and stress—the very things that helped keep you safe back then when you weren't sure how else to navigate life?"[1]

And then, one step at a time, my calves started to feel a sweet relief. Jess's pace was shifting as her body started to ease off the gas pedal.

Jess's voice quieted as she responded, "I guess this part of me doesn't really know that. She thinks I'm still eighteen. She has no idea that nearly thirty years have gone by. She has no idea how hard I've worked or that I have a home and savings. She doesn't know I've become more than competent at my job and have options I didn't have back then."

Our pace continued to slow down, and we settled into a stroll that lulled our legs into more spacious steps. I watched and heard her whole body sigh. Then her eyes grew wide.

"Wow, I mean, I've never realized this before, but when I have a presentation coming up, my mindset really does jump that far back in the past. It's like I completely go back there, forgetting where I am in the present and what life is like now."

As we continued walking together that day and in the months ahead, I had a front-row seat to witness her movements shift. Her heels no longer struck the ground with an alarming amount of intensity, but instead they took more steps with an ease that yielded into the earth. Her speech no longer ran a mile a minute with her legs, but instead strolled along with the slower cadence of our steps. She was no longer driven by what was happening inside her but instead could hold and *be with* what was stirring within. She no longer felt like eighteen-year-old her was working *against* her. Instead, she started to work *with* and tend toward this part of herself.

Embodied Flexibility

We constantly move through a mixture of emotions in life—everything from fear, joy, pain, surprise, grief, rest, and panic to overwhelm and more. And across these experiences, our goal isn't to ensure that our neuroception never detects threats and that we keep our brake system engaged so our body remains at a constant standstill. What helps us cultivate the smoothest ride in life is learning to work with our neuroception, gas pedal, and brake system—and the parts of us that are intertwined with them—rather than being reactively moved through our days on autopilot.

The beautiful thing is that we are already designed for this kind of movement. Our brain and body know how to hold mixed states.[2] We are wired to be flexible—to move through states of safety, stress, and shutdown, as well as combinations of them. Because of our flexibility, we can both be anchored in safety and experience some of the energy of the gas pedal in a helpful and even therapeutic way.

This was a massive relief to the parts of me who didn't like to slow down into thirty minutes of silent meditation right away, parts of me who didn't know how to stop moving or keep my blood from pumping. These active, adventure-seeking parts didn't have to keep me from grounding in safety, or from pressing into growth and healing.

Think about playing a game with friends or family. If you're into the game and having fun, your system is likely enjoying a mixture of both safety and stress—anchored in the moment *and* activated by the gas pedal. This reminds us that our body pressing the gas pedal is not always a bad thing.

When I play a game of tag with my sisters' kids, I don't just gently tap on the gas. My body fully presses in, energized by adrenaline to chase my speedy nieces and nephews. Being fueled this intensely doesn't overwhelm my body. Instead, it's incredibly refreshing to run that fast and breathe that hard, all anchored in the contained safety of playing a game with loved ones.

One of the most beautiful aspects of this kind of full body play is the way it invites parts of us to literally move differently. This can create space for parts of ourselves to safely shift out of the muscle memory of reactive protective strategies that feel burdening, that tense our muscles and increase the heavy load of stress we carry.

If I'm running around in a game of tag, it's therapeutic for parts of me that have been activated from work stress to sweat out some toxins. When I'm running around like this, these parts of me know that I'm in a space where I get to simply run around and have fun. I don't have to do or perform. Rather than charging through life, I'm in a space where I can simply be in the present with precious faces who are smiling and laughing with me, cues to all parts of me that I am not alone and I am safe.

Along with unburdening parts of us that feel stuck in tension or protective strategies, play also invites more vulnerable parts of ourselves to peek their heads out and enjoy the present moment. In these kinds of spaces, we can step into the fullness of our embodied being, reaching beyond our thinking brain and into curious and creative facets inside, facets that might not connect with cognitive thoughts but can connect beneath words, with movement and play.

Maybe playing tag with kids sounds like a nightmare to you or isn't something your body can physically do right now. Maybe going dancing, taking a walk in the woods, playing a board game, or creating something with your hands would be a more natural place for parts of you to explore movement and play. Or your starting point might simply be imagining the possibility of inviting parts of you into play, being curious to notice if this feels accessible, desirable, confusing, or blocked in some way.

Or maybe you don't resonate with any of those possibilities, instead hearing a voice inside that's crying, *I'm too tired to even think about playing! I just want a nap!* When we are worn out and have been living in chronic stress, we're often most drawn to rest, and for good reason. When we're tired, play and movement don't always sound appealing because they require energy that we might not have. If this is where you find yourself, I hope you will allow yourself space for rest before you try to force movement and play that doesn't feel accessible yet. If parts of you want to play, and other parts feel you need to rest, you can strike a compromise. Consider splitting your time between playful movement and rest, or finding movement that feels restful and restorative.

PAUSE & PLAY:

FREE MOVEMENT

I'm curious: When you were a little kid, what were your favorite ways to move your body and play? What kinds of movements or stillness felt freeing and safe?

Were there games or sports that felt like a contained space for you to explore movement and fun with friends? If your childhood did not include memories like this, what do you imagine a fun game would have been to safely play with family or friends?

After reflecting on how you've experienced play in the past, consider what it might feel like to play in the now:

Do you imagine play having a place in your life right now? If not, what do you think would need to shift internally, or externally, to create spaces to play?

Let's explore dipping our toe into some play right now. Put on some music and see what it's like to freely move your body—choose a song that feels upbeat, makes you smile, or makes you want to move. As you start to move your body to the music, imagine shaking off stress and shaking out the muscle memory of protective strategies that are embedded inside.

Rather than trying to be a ballerina, consider letting your body sway, bounce, or jump in a way that feels authentic rather than choreographed. If that feels silly, see what it's like to let yourself smile and laugh, delighting in anything that initially feels ridiculous.

Next, imagine inviting different parts of you to take the dance floor. Rather than forcing any part of you to engage, simply be curious to notice which parts of you are quick to join the party and which aren't sold on this idea quite yet.

If it does not feel safe to move your body, see what it's like to imagine dancing, shaking, or swaying to music in your mind. If moving your body is not possible for any reason, honor what your body needs and do not force movement that might be harmful.

Mindful Movements

In the same way we can shift through autonomic states without thinking, we can move—whether we're walking, working out, or dancing—without consciously thinking about it. Exploring mindful movements can help anchor us in our body and explore new ways to navigate life.[3] Mindful movement can be thought of as simply being present with our body, connecting to movements, whether they're small, big, slow, fast, or subtle.

When we move mindfully, or get lost in play, we create space for our body to stretch flexibly across autonomic states, allowing us to connect with these shifts rather than being driven by them. And when we're connected to safety as we stretch ourselves into new movements, we have a remarkable access point, not only to dream about how we might work with our body to move through life differently, but also to take the risks of trying out new kinds of movements. Both mindful movement and play cultivate experiential spaces that can cushion us with safety to reach for new movements that otherwise might feel too vulnerable.

From the simplicity of breath to the rush of a sprint, or from the gentle motion of a slow stroll to a full body bounce in a dance, being in our body and with our body as we move cultivates a mindfulness that can ground us and regulate our entire being. Mindful embodiment of movements like yielding, pushing, reaching, holding, and pulling in safe and playful spaces can create a secure foundation that might even enable us to risk these new movements in other spaces—whether that be in our relationships, workplace, or faith community.

If we long to get unstuck, to work *with* what's happening inside us, these kinds of experiential risks are crucial. Without them, it's all too easy for us to cycle through what we have known, letting the past shape our future beneath the surface of our awareness.

This is why simply envisioning mental imagery related to what's happening inside can be so powerful—simply playing with the idea of how parts of us might be cared for can shift what we imagine as a possibility in the future.[4] A thought or mental image alone can be a first movement of tasting something new, of our parts seeing the world from a different viewpoint, which is why so many of our Pause & Play prompts have invited mental imagery, creating space to sketch out new possibilities.

For some people, this kind of active imagining[5] doesn't feel natural or might seem blocked in some way. Whether we connect more with sketching out something in the imagination of our mind, in a tangible experience, or some combination of the two, it all starts with trying out something new, which is risky.

I want to name and honor that no matter how many times we envision how to safely explore moving through life differently or how secure of a space we try something in, it's still possible that new movements will not go well. And when this happens—when we vulnerably take a risk and it seems to backfire—it's really easy for protective perspectives to react harshly. While I wish I could leave you with a three-step formula to avoid this, living wholeheartedly inherently includes vulnerability and risk.

We can't get rid of the possibility of feeling vulnerable, disappointed, or wounded when we take risks in life. Reaching for anything, whether it be a dream, a loved one, or communion with God, comes with no guarantee that we will experience holding and pulling something close in the ways we long to. Instead, we might be left feeling rejected, incompetent, unworthy, or any number of other unpleasant experiences that may flood our body and swirl self-shaming thoughts. Simply put, no matter what we do, we cannot control the outcome when we try new things. What we can do, regardless of outcomes, is to tend to what's happening within—consistently caring for the multifaceted whole of our being—across the messiness of life that will inevitably include a mixture of emotions and experiences.

Planting Seeds

I like to think of the long-term care of tending to the depths of our souls as tending to a garden or some other terrain. When we take care of a garden, we generally aren't only concerned with keeping the plants from withering but we also want to help them flourish. And before we carry on, I'm curious how the word *flourishing* sits with you—the idea of not just being well, but of beautifully thriving.

I remember noticing strong reactions inside me the first time I heard someone simply suggest the idea of flourishing in our spiritual formation. To be honest, years ago, something about the word *flourishing* provoked a concern inside. I wondered if it might be self-centered or greedy to long for or to press into flourishing. Old messages distorted how I heard this word in relation to spiritual formation, the shaping of a person created by God.

But then I realized that we don't look at other things God created, like blossoms and trees, and think they're being selfish when they thrive. We don't judge a well-watered flower bed for being self-consumed or vain for bursting with glorious colors. And we don't blame a withering leaf for not taking care of itself.[6] Instead, we understand that without enough sunlight, water, or nutrients in the soil, growth and well-being will be hindered. We also understand that different environments, climates, and weather patterns might influence the way we care for certain plants.

In the same way we can't stop the complexities of life from being messy, we can't stop the weather. But what we can do is care for plants across seasons and years, being mindful of how they're impacted by different kinds of weather. In East Tennessee, when temperatures drop below freezing, you'll often see bed sheets and tarps covering plants that can't survive these temperatures, something you'd never see happen in the summer. In the spring, when you see delicate pink dogwoods thriving, you know that the soil surrounding these trees has an ideal level of pH and that the mixture of sun and shade is just right. When we're invested in the long-term growth and flourishing of flowers or trees, we're mindful of these details.

And so, with a similar kind of mindful attunement to the gardens within, I wonder how we might approach our embodied being with tender care, helping the many facets inside weather the seasons and elements of life. In the same way we would water or move a withering plant into sunlight, I wonder, what might be the living water, light brighter than the sun, and sturdy ground for the neglected parts of us that need care? What might be the steadfast nourishment and security we need to take risks, providing what we need even when those risks don't work out so well?

As you consider these questions, I'm going to restate something I said in chapter 1: The pages in this book do not walk us through a linear journey from point A to point B. All of our prompts have been strung together loosely so you have space to circle back to the ones you'd like to spend more time with or consider from different points of view. Maybe you feel like you need to go back to some earlier chapters before engaging with this chapter fully, or maybe this chapter provides what you need so you can go back to earlier chapters that previously felt disconnected. Wherever you find yourself, my hope is that you'll feel inspired to continue curiously exploring what a deeper connection with your internal world might look like.

For any part of you that's reading this and wondering, *Wait—we can't be done, I still don't know how to actually do this stuff we've been talking about!*, I've put together additional resources that you'll find after these chapters. "Stringing It All Together" on page 179 brings each chapter together in one space so you can engage with the prompts and concepts from the book cohesively. And if you're longing for more exercises like the Pause & Play prompts in each chapter, you can find additional ones in "Pause Longer & Play Harder" on page 193.

Before we close this last chapter, I invite you to imagine how you'll continue to care for the whole of your embodied being with the prompts below. You might even get curious about how this tending might intersect with your relationships with other people, joining together to care for the fullness of who we are, not just as separate individuals, but as people who are connected by relationships, families, and communities.

However you envision the garden within, may your roots grow deep and find the nourishment they need. May your buds and leaves blossom brilliantly. May there be a glorious chorus of bird songs accompanied by the pitter-patter of scampering creatures dancing and playing around you. May you whimsically sway with the breeze and delight in the warmth of the sun. And may all these things provide what you need for the days that are dark, the seasons that are dry, and the losses that change the landscape within. In all the elements, and across seasons, may you experience a beautiful and restorative newness, joining with the One who created all things, who longs to make all things new and right.

PAUSE & PLAY:

GARDENING WITHIN

In your imagination or on a piece of paper, sketch a flower bed or an orchard. Include plants, flowers, and trees that represent different parts of you. Give yourself permission not to worry about how artistic your drawing is. See what it's like to invite young and creative parts of you to join with you in this exercise.

In your flower bed or orchard, consider including a plant to represent each of the following:

- A part of you that takes the driver's seat to move through life, whether going to work, picking up groceries, or paying your bills
- A part of you that most people don't know or see, one that feels tucked away and forgotten either by you or by others
- A part of you that is free to savor life when you are on vacation or enjoying a three-day weekend
- A part of you that gets overwhelmed with anxiety, anger, or people-pleasing
- A part of you that represents a younger part of you, the most beloved and playful part of yourself that you can think of
- Any other part of you that comes to mind

As you sketch each plant representing a part of you, see what it's like to consider the ways they are withering or thriving. Ask yourself:

> *Is everyone getting enough sun? What might sunlight represent in their growth?*
>
> *Is everyone getting enough water? What might water represent in their needs?*
>
> *Does everyone have enough nutrients in the soil beneath them? What might soil represent in their nourishment?*
>
> *Are bird songs or music playing around the plants? What might these melodies represent in the joy of their flourishing?*

In the same way that you might put together a plan to care for a garden, how do you want to tend to this garden in the present season you are in? Ask yourself:

> *What might it look like for me to check on how each plant is doing? How might different parts of me need a different kind of check-in?*
>
> *How can I prepare these plants for weeks or trips where I might not have as much time to tend to them? How might I invite others to be parts of tending to the terrain of my soul?*
>
> *What types of blossoms or other signs of flourishing do I long to see in the coming months? What kind of care might these plants need in order to thrive?*
>
> *Do I want to imagine God in this garden? If so, where in the garden, and with what kind of movement or engagement?*
>
> *What kind of prayer or psalm might express my longings for this garden? How might I invite God to tend to these plants in a prayer or a psalm?*

afterword

I hope these pages have brought you into a deeper connection with the whole of your created being, bringing to life what has been forgotten beneath the surface. And as you continue the lifelong journey of slowing down, tuning in with your body, and tending to the depths of your soul, may you remember that you can take all the time you need, that you are not alone, and that you have choices for how you move through life.

May the continual work of caring for all that is within you extend to transforming relationships and communities around you. May the new experiences of safety you step into cultivate bridges so you can offer your presence, and receive the presence of others, with an open heart that's linked with an attuned face. And may the movements you explore and embody invite others into new movements alongside you, inspiring the hope of renewal that sometimes doesn't feel possible.

In the ways you still feel stuck or as if you're still working against yourself, may there be a dawning hope that maybe, just maybe, you will be able to interact differently with what stirs inside you. May there be an image inside of what that could possibly look like, even if it feels like the most remotely hypothetical thing you've ever imagined.

In the ways you simply feel exhausted and disconnected from hope, may there be a glimmer of possibility that maybe, just maybe, a journey of restoration could lie ahead. As you continue to tend to the depths inside, I hope you will reach for new experiences of safety that aren't anchored solely in rest but include free and flexible movements that spur on play and cultivate flourishing.

And now, while there are so many more things I would love to say and share with you in this space, just as fixed words on a page limit me from being physically present with you, those words are limited to the fixed time of writing and printing deadlines. You're holding the words that were sent on a final deadline, words that were the best way I knew to communicate what I wanted to say as I worked on these drafts.

And on this day, in this moment, if I could boil it all down to one (lengthy!) sentence, this is what I want to say:

Every facet of your entire embodied being is sacred, and no matter how any of those strands has been forgotten or dismissed, you are always welcome to join me in slowing down, tuning in, and tending toward everything that is within us, all for the purpose of creating something beautiful and new with those around us—loving more deeply, moving more freely, and being alive to all we were created for as we embody and inspire restoration, presence, and peace.

We have always known how to do this.

Thank you for walking with me. ♥

acknowledgments

I cannot remember the books I've read any more than
the meals I have eaten; even so, they have made me.

ATTRIBUTED TO RALPH WALDO EMERSON

I've loved these words since I first heard them—the way they speak to how we are shaped, not only by the things we can recall, but also by implicit legacies that are ever molding the person we are becoming. Along with the books I've read, the interactions and experiences of my life are remembered both implicitly and explicitly—stored in my body and the person I am today, and sometimes seared in my memory like one of the best meals I've ever eaten or one of the worst.

And as much as I sometimes wish I could forget strands of my story that I never asked to walk, I know that I would not be the person I am today apart from every meal, every book, every joy, and every sorrow that I have encountered, regardless of how my body does or does not remember each of them. And in and through my life, there have been countless friends, family, found family, therapists, mentors, professors, supervisors, trainers, clients, and others who have intersected with pivotal moments and seasons, leaving legacies within me that I'm confident run far beyond what I'm able to trace. I am grateful for the joy and the sorrow that have been stitched together to make me who I am today—and for each person who has been woven into that story—helping me become the me who wrote the words you're holding in your hands today. So, to anyone and everyone who has left an imprint on my life, thank you.

And to those who have so explicitly—and so kindly—encouraged me and supported me from the time I was only playing with the idea of crafting these pages, thank you for walking this wild journey with me. While it would require another book to thank everyone appropriately, in these short pages, I want to specifically thank . . .

Elijah, for believing in me and my dreams from the time we were just friends in seminary along with your patient listening ear that has heard me process the ideas in these pages for years. I didn't intend to write a book about slowing down, and as I reflect on that being what came together here, I know that you have been my greatest experiential teacher on this subject. Every day of our lives you invite me into a slower pace—one that is calm, has space for deep breaths, is tenderly unrushed, and is anchored in presence. Thank you for being a steady rock ever beside me, supporting me in more ways than I can count. For every meal, snack, smoothie, back rub, and hug you have nourished me with to keep me going in this project, thank you.

Rachel, for relentlessly telling me for years that I needed to write a book and that I had something to say. I honestly don't know if I would have ever started playing with publishing apart from your persistence and belief in me.

Mary, for cheering me on with an unparalleled and loyal fierceness that fueled me to put words to paper when I was tired and ready to give up. You saw my drive and spoke life into my longing that was burning out. You being you, and being the pinkest of friends, carried me and stayed with me through this whole process. Thank you.

Julia, for helping me balance screen fatigue with mountain adventures. You pushed me to work hard, knowing our hikes would be a place where I could play harder. Thank you for bringing out such a sweet playfulness in me at all times, and especially in the thick of writing these chapters. I would not have been able to so authentically access certain facets of myself without the rhythm of our explorations and play that shaped the cadence of my writing weeks.

My family, for celebrating with me as I've taken this project on, speaking belief into my ability to carry it out despite the fact that it was entirely new to me. Mom, for embodying such a curious creativity, regularly and boldly exploring new crafts throughout your life.

Your example has spurred me on to do the same. Dad, for passing on a memory and quick wit that I can see woven into my writing. Laura, for always celebrating the small and big things with me in life. I cherish how as adults, our younger selves can still find each other in childlike excitement. Ross, for making time to hop into an abandoned field to take incredible headshots in between the nuggets' soccer, ballet, and swim lessons. Jen and Joe, for correcting my grammar and syntax for years and playfully pushing me intellectually. My sweet nieces and nephews, for your interest and curiosity about what I've been writing and what this book will be. Your presence, joy, love, brilliance, and kindness inspire me every day.

Kristy, for reading an early draft of this manuscript and so thoughtfully journeying with my words. Stephanie, for reminding me of my own words, and what I already knew—and always have known—how to do. And all my sacred fem friends, thank you for holding me through months of writing and transition that could have been so much scarier and lonelier without you.

My clients, for letting me in to see the depths of your humanity in beautifully sacred ways. Thank you for allowing me to journey alongside you, accepting me as I was—not a blank slate, but a deeply feeling human. I would not be the person I am today without walking alongside each one of you. Thank you for teaching me and for being such a unique part of shaping who I am.

Chuck, for hearing me and seeing me from our very first conversations. You caught the vision of what I wanted to say in a book and have so graciously supported my words coming to fruition in this way. Thank you.

Those who took time out of incredibly busy schedules to read this manuscript and offer words of endorsement, thank you. Your support is a gift that I do not take for granted.

The whole team that has seen this project through at Tyndale, thank you for everything—both what I've known and what I haven't seen behind the scenes—to support all of this coming together so beautifully. Jillian, for hearing my voice and advocating for this manuscript from our first conversation. Thank you for encouraging me in finding my own way through the writing process rather than trying to fit me into a cookie-cutter mold. You'll never know how much that has meant to me. Kim, for handling this manuscript with such tender care. You so gracefully honored my voice and my words. Having you as a conversation partner helped me say what I wanted to say so much more clearly. Thank you. Lindsey, for giving me categories to envision how I longed to translate the invitation of this book into a cover design, and Libby, for seeing what I was dreaming up and bringing it to fruition. Thank you.

The growing community that has backed my writing and work on Substack, thank you for believing in me and affirming that what I long to share matters.

To the men and women who have devoted their lives to understanding what's happening in our internal worlds—making sense of the wounds we carry with us and how to tend to these in the most humane ways—thank you for shaping me as a human and a therapist. I would not be who I am today, nor would I have written this book without the work of so many—most especially Janina Fisher, Sue Johnson, Daniel Siegel, Stephen Porges, and Deb Dana. And Marva Dawn, whose work is what first inspired me to pursue my two master's degrees—your brilliance and tenderness showed me that you don't need to dumb things down when connecting at a heart level, and you don't need to disconnect the heart from heady content. I also wish we could have been colleagues and treasure the brief chance we had to intersect.

And now, lastly, while certainly not the least to thank: To the One who I have to believe holds all things together, even through pain and heartache that I can't make sense of, thank You. In the mysteriousness of life, I don't know the intricacies of how this writing project was allowed, orchestrated, or ordained—but I do know this: I am not the same person I was when I first submitted this publishing proposal, and I see You forming me in ways that leave me in awe and wonder. From the time I wrote in journals as a young teenager, thank You for drawing me into a gentle pace and anchored spaces with You—to the fields with windmills to slow down, into the woods with trees to get grounded, to the top of literal and figurative mountains to gain new perspectives, and into the gentle lull of a swinging hammock to settle into simplicity. Thank You for creating so many beautiful things in and around me, especially out of spaces that at times have felt so lifeless and beyond repair—and thank You for inviting us to join You in making all things new.

ἀμήν

additional resources

stringing it all together

A Linear Guide to a Nonlinear Journey

If you have found yourself wanting a linear set of tracks to run on that brings these pages together, then this section is for you! I've written this resource to offer something a bit more concrete and cohesive that strings each chapter of the book together in one place. While I don't want to give the impression that this will guide you through a neat and tidy point A to point B process, I also know there are parts of us that sometimes need clear direction when trying something new. You can consider these prompts as a scaffolding of support to continue to explore the concepts in each chapter. Grab a journal and take all the time and space you need to move through each paragraph and page.

Please know that it is completely normal to cycle through these prompts at different speeds and in various orders, and to have the journey feel like a nonlinear path with surprises along the way. I invite you to take what you long for and need from these words, not holding yourself to a standard of what this *should* look like. It is completely normal to spend multiple hours across several days working through all the reflections that follow.

Starting Prompt

Consider a space in your life where you feel frustrated or stuck, as though there's a disconnect you can't quite figure out how to get past. Reflect on scenarios when you feel like you're working against yourself and wish that things could look different.

- Maybe the same conflict seems to keep cycling in a relationship and you'd like to figure out how to resolve it.
- Maybe your spiritual life feels empty or disconnected from God, but any attempts to go deeper don't seem to be working.
- Maybe you feel trapped in a role at work, with friends, or with family, but you have no idea how to break out of it.
- Maybe you've been going to therapy and reading recommended books. And even though you felt encouraged early on, you feel defeated when everything you're learning seems to go out the window as soon as __________________________________ happens. What's the fill-in-the-blank scenario that happens?

Once you have identified a specific life-example to focus on, write or draw a brief summary of the scenario before continuing on.

After writing or drawing what this situation presently looks like in your life, write or draw what you *wish* things looked like instead. Imagine if you woke up in a hypothetical world tomorrow and the issues you're facing were no longer there. If the problem was gone, how would you know? What would look different in your life? What would feel different inside?[1] Write or draw a depiction of this.

Now, at your own pace, taking breaks as you want or need to, continue with the prompts that follow. Each starts with reflection questions to consider, along with options for how you might journey through the themes of each chapter as you explore the many facets of your life-example.

You can go through these prompts as many times as you like. I recommend working with only one life-example at a time, and moving through these questions *slowly*.

Please note: If at any time you feel overwhelmed by these prompts, I invite you to pause, use the grounding exercises on pages 24–25, and consider whether you might set this resource aside until you are able to bring it to a trusted person, such as a therapist, to help you unpack what's stirring within.

If this seems best, while you wait to be able to bring this to a trusted other, consider imagining a safe person or animal sitting with you, holding you in your overwhelm.

Reflecting on chapter 1, ask yourself: *How do I feel about connecting with what's going on beneath my thinking brain, and my body specifically?*

With a deep breath, give yourself time and space to survey your starting point. Are you feeling energized or exhausted from your day so far? Do you long to begin working through these prompts, or do you worry you should be doing something else right now? Is the example you've picked out something you feel comfortable exploring alone, or would you like to bring this to a safe space, such as with a therapist?

Reflecting on chapter 2, ask yourself: *Do I notice any resistance to slowing down and getting in touch with what's happening inside? In what ways does this feel risky, threatening, or inconvenient?*

See what it's like to hold silence and simply be for a moment. How is this sitting with you? Would it feel better to do ten jumping jacks before you slow down, or to go for a walk to move with some emotions before sitting with them? Would it be helpful to remind yourself that if slowing down becomes too uncomfortable, you have freedom to pause and come back to this at another time?

To move with your body as you slow down: Consider if there is a certain song you could listen to that invites your internal world to take a deep breath and feel settled. See what it's like to gently sway your body with this song, not trying to dance in a performative way but to move in an authentic and free-flowing way. Maybe your body needs to shake and jump around before you slow down. Maybe your body wants to lie flat on the ground or curl up in a ball. See what it's like to follow the shapes your body naturally takes as you slow down.

Explore some deep breathing: Inhale for four counts, hold your breath for four counts, and then slowly exhale for eight counts. See what it's like to place your hands over your heart, abdomen, jaw, or neck, connecting with your body as you breathe in and out. Experiment with making loud noises as you breathe out—anything from sighing to nearly roaring, releasing stress or tension as you settle in. If deep breathing prompts panic or frustration, do not force a specific cadence with your inhale and exhale.

Reflecting back on chapter 3, ask yourself: *What happens in my body when I think about this life-example? How would I fill in a body outline worksheet to depict what's happening inside? Which emotions would be present, and how would they be represented in my body?*

With your hands over your heart, abdomen, shoulders, legs, or the ground (or anywhere else that feels most safe!), what is your body telling you right now? What feedback would your body like to offer? Even if it feels super silly, see what it's like to ask your body, *What's happening inside right now?*

If you can't put it into verbal language (words), see what it's like to imagine and draw what is stirring inside. Consider drawing this on a blank piece of paper or in a body outline like the one on page 48, exploring shapes, symbols, and colors as expressions of what is happening within.

If you feel you need words to explore this, consider searching for a feelings wheel online, picking words and categories that express the emotions you are feeling inside.

Consider how what's happening in your body in this moment is similar to or different from when you are engaged in the life-example you're focusing on.

Reflecting on chapter 4, ask yourself: *What is my initial reaction as I listen to what is stirring within? Does it feel like noise I would rather tune out, or can I imagine this as a part of me that's hoping I might listen in?*

Place your hands on your body or a surface around you, closing your eyes for a moment. See how you might envision what's happening inside of you in terms of a part of you. This might be a younger version of you, an animal (like a crying kitten), or any other depiction that represents what is stirring inside in an embodied image.

Ask yourself, *If my internal world were a house, where would this part of me be in the house? Forgotten, locked away behind closed doors? Clawing at a door to get out? Silently staying in the dark, having given up?*

Notice how it feels to imagine these stirrings as noise in contrast with how it feels to imagine these stirrings as a facet of your being. Does it feel different? If so, how?

Consider asking this part of you, *What would you like me to hear? What would you like me to know?* If it feels helpful, you can draw this conversation out, even if it's just with stick figures, giving this part of you speech and thought bubbles.

Reflecting on chapter 5, ask yourself: *In what ways do I feel the gas and the brakes pressed inside? Do I feel a surge of anxiety or stress? Do I feel stopped in my tracks or like I'm going to explode or crumble? Are the movements within this life-example abrupt or subtle? Fueled or flattened?*

Notice the energy and movement of what's stirring within. Consider moving your body in an external expression of this, running around the house if you feel the gas pedal pressed inside, or sitting stationary if you feel the brakes locked on.

Notice how you are sensing the gas and brakes inside. Do you sense these internal movements in your thoughts, emotions, memories, somatic sensations, or any other way? How are these internal movements in or out of sync with each other?

How does the movement in your internal world in this moment differ from the movement in your internal world when you are in the life-example you're focusing on?

Reflecting on chapter 6, ask yourself: *Where in the autonomic landscape (safety, stress, or shutdown) am I right now? How am I moving in or through this terrain? Am I in just one state, a mixture of two, or cycling through different states?*

As you continue to slow down and tune in with your body, notice how the feedback inside is connected to your autonomic states.

Maybe the state you are in right now differs from the autonomic state that's connected to your life-example. If these states are different, how are they distinct? How can you sense that you are in a different state in this moment than the state you are in when you are in the life-example?

Which state(s) do you wish you could be in during this life-example? What do you think you would need in order for you to have enough safety to move through your autonomic landscape differently when this life-example comes up?

In what ways do you shame yourself for what happens at this autonomic level? In what ways might you offer yourself curiosity and compassion about what happens at this autonomic level? For example, consider:

> *I wonder what drives me to this place.*
>
> *I wonder how my body believes entering or staying in this state might help me.*

Reflecting on chapter 7, ask yourself: *Which protective strategies are moving me and shaping my perspective? What elevations of safety, stress, or shutdown are these protective strategies moving me through? How do these protective strategies handle these elevations?*

I invite you to consider holding or hugging your body, wrapping yourself in a blanket, or snuggling up with a real or stuffed animal, as you reflect on these protective strategies.

After taking a deep breath and shaking or moving around if it feels helpful, consider which protective strategies pop up during your life-example. Curiously ask yourself:

When this life-example happens, do I . . .

> *Fight? Charge ahead to tackle what's in front of me or combat the person across from me?*
>
> *Flee? Try to get out of the scenario, whether it's in thought or action?*
>
> *Fawn? Keep the peace to try to not rock the boat until I make it through?*
>
> *Find? Seek out some sort of connection or protection to help me feel secure?*
>
> *Freeze? Feel paralyzed as my body and thoughts go rigid, unable to move?*
>
> *Flop? Collapse as my body and thoughts go unresponsive, possibly even leading me to faint?*
>
> *Fragment? Disconnect from the present, detaching from my body in order to survive?*

How do you feel toward yourself as you identify the ways you protectively react in this life-example? Critical? Curious? Compassionate?

Inserting the protective strategy or strategies you've identified above, see what it's like to pause and consider:

When I ____,
how does this shape the perspective of the part of me that's in the driver's seat?

I wonder how this protective strategy helped me in the past, and how this part of me believes it's helping me right now.

Note: You might find that there seem to be competing protective strategies stirring beneath the surface, with different parts of you reaching for control of the steering wheel.

Reflecting on chapter 8, ask yourself: *How might understanding the story that informs my movements in this life-example shift my posture toward my reactions? What makes it difficult for me to be curious about this life-example? Is there a critical voice inside that pushes against getting curious?*

Notice whether an inner critic is chiming in on your reflections here. If so, see what it's like to ask this part of you to give you some breathing room to try this exercise. This isn't a matter of shaming the inner critic away. Instead, you're just asking for some space to try something new. The inner critic can remain skeptical if that's how they feel.

Consider how you imagine this inner critic part of you. What is their posture like? What about their tone and facial expression? See what it's like to imagine having a conversation with this part of you.

Let the inner critic know that you are on the same team. See what it's like to understand the perspective of this inner critic, asking them how they believe it helps you to be critical, judgmental, or shaming.

Once you feel the inner critic is willing to give you breathing room to move through these prompts, continue on below. While it might seem strange, you can simply imagine asking this part of you for what you need.

With curiosity and compassion, which you can imagine borrowing from me or any other person if you can't find it in yourself at this moment, see what it's like to ask yourself the following:

What story has shaped how I move through this life-example?

If I could give someone a book that would explain why I act the way I do in this life-example, what would it be about?

If I were to ask the part(s) of me that come alive in this life-example why they act as they do, what would they want me to know? What might they say?

How are my movements trying to keep me safe? What in the past has shaped my perspective and informed protective reactions that are prompted inside? How does the way I'm wired shape my perspective and inform protective reactions that are prompted inside?

Reflecting on chapter 9, ask yourself: *What different movements do I long to see myself explore in this life-example? What movements can I not even imagine myself being able to explore in this life-example?*

Find a place to comfortably sit or lie on the ground, or if it's better for your body, find a different position on another surface. As you hold a connection to the part(s) of you that come alive in this life-example, see what it's like to play with the following reflections. Remember, these movements are related to both the ways we explored the world when we were little, and the ways we move through life and relationships now. You might explore literal or metaphorical movements, such as reaching for a loved one or reaching for a dream.

Yield*—How do I imagine this part of me yielding? Does this part of me feel freedom to yield, sinking into simply existing or being? Does this part of me hold tension, unable to fully relax? What kind of safety might this part of me need to explore yielding more freely?*

Push*—How do I imagine this part of me pushing? Does this part of me feel permission to push? If this part of me does push, does it happen in a way that seems anchored in security, fear, survival, or freedom? What kind of safety might this part of me need to explore pushing more freely?*

Reach*—How do I imagine this part of me reaching? Does this part of me feel freedom to reach for what I long for and most need? If this part of me does* *reach, does it happen in a way that seems fueled by security, fear, survival, and/or freedom? What kind of safety might this part of me need to explore reaching more freely?*

Hold and Pull—*How do I imagine this part of me holding and pulling? Does this part of me feel freedom to hold on to and pull close what I reach for? How do any complications in reaching impact the ways that this part of me holds on to and pulls close what I reach for? What kind of safety might this part of me need to explore holding and pulling more freely?*

Reflecting back on chapter 10, ask yourself: *In what ways does the thought of moving toward safety, as it relates to this life-example, not feel safe at a gut level? What feels vulnerable about inviting parts of me into new movements that are anchored in safety? What raw or painful wounds have gotten tangled up in the story that pops up with this life-example? In what ways is vulnerability associated with that story?*

Continuing with the reflections from the previous chapter, let's slow down and survey what kinds of safety you might need to develop in order to explore new movements. Consider going back to the inner-critic reflections from the chapter 8 reflections if you find yourself shaming or judging yourself.

With a deep breath, see what it's like to let your body take the shape of what happens in this life-example. Extend, contract, gesture, or move in ways that externally express how your body sinks into, or moves away from, a sense of anchored safety.

Without forcing your body into any other posture, curiously consider what your body might need as you ask yourself:

What is the safety my body might need to explore yielding here—sinking into the present? What is one small thing I can do this week to offer this sense of safety to my body?

What is the safety my body might need to explore pushing—moving toward or away from what I long for or need? What is one small thing I can do this week to offer this sense of safety to my body?

What is the safety my body might need to explore reaching—seeking out what I long for or need? What is one small thing I can do this week to offer this sense of safety to my body?

What is the safety my body might need to explore holding—embracing what I long for or need? What is one small thing I can do this week to offer this sense of safety to my body?

What is the safety my body might need to explore pulling—bringing close what I long for or need? What is one small thing I can do this week to offer this sense of safety to my body?

As you explore increasing safety in each of these ways, see what it's like (without using force) to play with moving your body through the motions of yielding, pushing, reaching, holding, and pulling.

Before moving on, take a moment to mindfully consider how you might tend to any lack of safety, or compromised safety, that is in need of repair. In what ways can you continue to invest in increasing safety for your body and the parts of you that come alive in your life-example?

Reflecting on chapter 11, ask yourself: *In what ways might I attune with the part of myself that comes alive in this life-example? How does it feel to explore inviting God to attune with this part of me?*

Either by drawing in your notebook or reflecting with your eyes closed, let your mind sketch out how you envision the "you" that comes alive in the life-example you're focusing on. Now imagine that you are offering your presence, the attunement of your face and body, to this part of you.

What happens inside as you imagine this? Does this bring relief? Feel overwhelming? Vulnerable? Beautiful?

Does it feel accessible to hug or hold yourself, or wrap yourself in a blanket or the snuggles of a furry friend?

Note: If you want to explore spiritual integration with this reflection, continue on with the following prompts. If not, go to the next chapter reflection.

As you continue to let your mind be curious and envision the part of you that comes alive in the life-example, what is it like to imagine that God is also present with this version of yourself?

Does God seem distant? Nearby? Can you imagine God's face attuning with this part of you? Do you imagine some sort of barrier between God and this part of you?

What does this part of you long for? Would this part of you like to explore any of the following movements? Consider imagining or drawing any of these that you would like to play with:

- Yielding in God's compassionate presence
- Pushing against assumptions or ideas about God that are contrary to God's heart
- Reaching for God's nearness
- Holding God's embrace, love, or grace near your heart
- Pulling God's light, mercy, or warmth toward you and holding it tightly

Reflecting on chapter 12, ask yourself: *What kind of movement would I like to explore as I continue to move with the life-example I've been focusing on? What might the various facets of me—mind, body, soul, heart, and more, all wrapped up in my one embodied being—need in order to be cared for, maybe even to the point of flourishing one day?*

Consider playing music that might encourage you to dance or bounce around, something that might even make you smile and laugh a little. See what it's like to invite the part of you that you've been focusing on to dance with you. You can place a hand over your heart and abdomen, inviting all that's stirring within to take a deep breath and enjoy some silly dancing.

Imagine sitting down with the "you" that you've been focusing on in this life-example. What might happen if you approached this part of you and said, "Let's get out of here and do something fun!" What would this part of you want to do? What's a way you can press into play?

If you're having a hard time thinking of playful activities, think back to ways you played as a child or consider looking through children's books that might depict various kinds of play and curiosity.

Drawing on the plant imagery from this chapter, what does your embodied being most need to be cared for as you continue on in the weeks ahead? What would the metaphorical water, sunshine, and nutrients in the soil be for this part of you? What does each of those necessities represent?

Can you imagine a day, even if it's far in the future, when this part of you is cared for so well that you not only move differently, but might even flourish? What is it like to hypothetically imagine something like this? How do you want to care for this part of you today as you hold that hope for the future in mind?

pause longer & play harder

More Opportunities to Slow Down, Tune In, and Tend Within

If you would like more opportunities to Pause & Play, then this section is for you! Enjoy exploring additional ways you can slow down, tune in with the body, and tend to the soul.

Exploring Emotions

See what it's like to explore the way you express each of the emotions below in your body through movement. Embodying experiential movements is a powerful way to connect with emotions and wake up to the fullness of what stirs inside. It can also feel silly or foreign. If you have little ones in your life—such as children, nieces, or nephews—consider inviting them to try this with you.

If prompts are helpful rather than starting with a blank slate, consider moving through the cues listed with each emotion. If your body would like to express these emotions in any other way, feel free to move with what's naturally stirring within.

Sadness

Sit on the ground or in a chair with your shoulders slumped forward, your face looking down, and your head leaning forward. Frown and close your eyes. Place your head in your hands. Wrap your arms around your legs, holding yourself in a ball. See how it feels to hold yourself here. Imagine or try sighing to express sadness. Instead of using words, see what it's like to explore other noises that communicate sadness.

Happiness

Skip around, playing with how it feels to smile, first with a small smirk and then as wide a smile as you can express. Try to smile with your eyes and the rest of your face, excluding your mouth. Notice what feels like your most natural smile, one depicting pure joy and glee rather than one you might wear when posing for a picture. Place a hand over your heart and your gut and laugh. Even if it's a fake laugh (making *ha-ha* and *he-he* noises), see how this affects your breathing and your smile, both the smile of your mouth and the smile of your entire face.

Fear

Tense your core muscles, along with the muscles in your legs, shoulders, neck, and jaw. Lift your hands abruptly in a self-protective posture. Try to stay frozen in this tension for a few moments. Then, one motion at a time, see what it's like to move back slowly. You can also try walking or running to see what it's like to let your body get away. Notice how it feels to stay frozen in contrast with how it feels to move. Play with letting your voice make a noise that communicates fear. If this doesn't feel natural, see what it's like to imitate the scared noises of a child, animal, or character from a TV show or movie.

Anger

Let yourself sigh or scoff, making an angry or annoyed sound as you furrow your eyebrows. Wrap your hands into fists, pushing them down toward the earth. Stomp your feet and yell. Notice if it feels difficult to let yourself feel or imitate anger. Play with increasing and decreasing the volume of your stomping and yelling, seeing what feels more or less comfortable for your body. As you play with anger, notice if your body feels warmer, and if so, where.

Disgust

Squint or roll your eyes. Open your mouth and say "Ew!" or "Ugh!" As you say this, let your head and upper body move back, as though you're moving away from something that's repulsive. See if the rest of your body wants to move back as well, noticing what naturally happens with your hands and arms during this movement.

Excitement

Breathe in suddenly, propelling your chest to rise abruptly. See what kind of sound comes out with this kind of breath, possibly something like "Oh!" or "Wow!" or "What?" Open your eyes wide and see if it feels natural to reactively place your hands in front of your mouth or on your head, as though you're a little kid who can't contain their excitement. Be curious to notice how your feet and the rest of your body want to react to being excited. Notice how playing with excitement feels similar to or different from the other emotions above.

Parts in a House

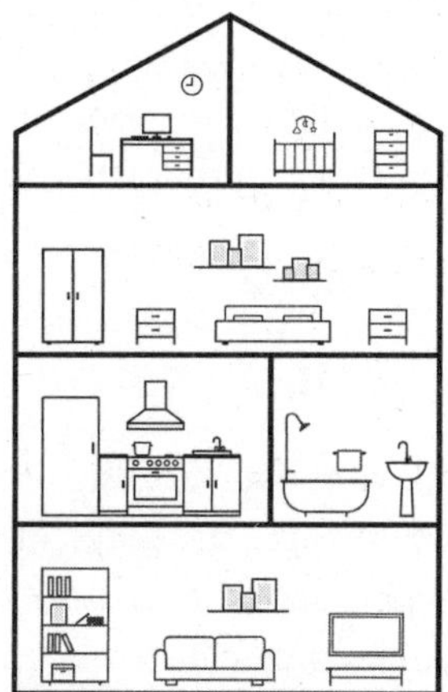

In your journal, draw a simple outline of a house layout or floor plan like the one above. Imagine that the rooms in this house represent your embodied being. Be curious about where different parts of you live in this house. Are young or scared parts of you tucked away in a closet or the crawl space? Who is the version of yourself that you consider the main "you," and what is their main living area? Are there any parts of you who are crying, frozen, or numb in a room that's closed off or barricaded in some way?

When life is too much and parts of you are overwhelmed, where do those parts go in the house? When parts of you can fully rest and breathe, where are they and how do they move through the house? Is anyone outside in the yard, on the roof, or trying to get out a window? Let your mind be playful and curious, simply noticing any imagery that naturally pops into your mind in response to these questions as you sketch out stick figures or caricatures of these parts of yourself.

After placing different parts of yourself in the home, consider:

> How have people in your life treated each of these parts of you? Which of their or your embedded beliefs resulted in shame or criticism toward any parts of you?
>
> Can you imagine viewing all parts of you with a new posture, like the compassionate perspectives listed at the end of chapter 4 (pages 57–58)? Which parts would be hardest to treat with this kind of tender care? What emotions come up as you think about the difference it makes to hold a different view of any parts of yourself?

Embodied Gas Pedal and Brake System

How do you resonate with your body gearing up to go, whether in excitement or stress? Let your body take the shape of what stirs within as you consider facing the following scenarios. Move your body in an external expression of what happens inside when:

- You're running late and rushing to get out of the house.

- You're sitting still in a meeting while your heart pounds with anxiety.
- You're anticipating something exciting you can't wait for, like a kid on Christmas morning. You feel like you're going to burst!

How do you resonate with your body slowing down, whether it's in freedom or overwhelm? Let your body take the shape of what stirs within in the following scenarios:

- You're so exhausted that you're about to collapse on the floor.
- You're settling down for a nap on vacation. No one needs you and you are free to rest.
- You've been shocked or scared and feel like you can't move, but you feel the rigidity of stress keeping your body upright.

Elevations of Stress

Draw out a simple sketch of a mountain range, like the one above. Sea level represents no stress, and mountain peaks represent high levels of stress. Below sea level represents so much stress, you feel like you're sinking underwater, with your body shutting down. On your image, place elevation markers for the places where you experience these different kinds of stress:

- Low-level stress: feels manageable
- Midrange stress: sustainable for a short period of time
- High-level stress: not sustainable, fueled by survival
- Elevation of intolerable stress: can't function—tumble down and sink into the sea

Next, consider the following questions and where you would plot out each answer:

- Where in the mountain range of stress do I start the beginning of each day?
- What are the things in life that can knock me down to crash into the sea?
- What helps me come back to sea level? When was the last time I felt anchored at sea level?

Tracing the Vulnerability of Safety

Use the following prompt to journal, draw, or write a dialogue:

> *If a protective perspective inside me were to explain the function of pressing the gas pedal or slamming the brakes instead of lulling me to yield into safety, they would say* ______________________.
>
> *In other words, how would these parts of me explain why pushing on the gas pedal or slamming on the brakes keeps me safer than yielding into safety? What is the function or strategy of this internal movement?*

Rather than judging or arguing with the body logic you're exploring, see what it's like to simply notice the feedback you receive. Try to understand the function of what happens internally from the perspective of protective strategies.

Inner-Critic Exploration

Find a comfortable spot to explore the guided imagery below, focusing on a part of you that seems to function as an inner critic.

You can imagine this part of you as a version of yourself, an animal, a television character, or any other representation that works for you, regardless of how silly it seems. Take time to close your eyes if this helps you sketch out how you envision this part of you.

Once you have decided how you'll imagine this part of you, notice what happens in your body as you consider the following reflections:

> *Is this part of me pressing on the gas or the brakes? How does this impact what I'm feeling in my body?*
>
> *What is this part of me worried about? What might happen if this part of me didn't anxiously push the gas or the brakes? How might that be risky or put me in a vulnerable position?*
>
> *What does this part of me most want? What does safety feel like to this part of me? Does all of me buy into their view of safety?*

See what it's like to ask this part of you if they are weary from holding their post and trying to keep you safe all the time.

Ask this part of you if they are open to considering ways they can rest while still being sure you will be safe. Consider going on a walk or journaling as you reflect on the ways you might work *with* this part of you toward the goal you both want—your overall well-being and safety.

Face-Presence

Solo option

In a screen-filled culture, I'm curious how the idea of our face and presence being so interconnected sits with you. With unending lists of emails and tasks that demand our face and presence day in and day out, it can feel like there's no margin to offer this kind of face-presence to others in our lives, let alone the parts that live inside us. It can feel like we're up against an impossible equation.

For just a minute, find an object, ideally something from outside to connect a bit with nature, and then *be with* this object for that minute. If you have more time, great! *Be with* the object for five minutes.

Notice what happens inside you when your *face* and *presence* are directed toward this one thing in this one place.

If your mind wanders, simply notice this.

If your eyes have difficulty focusing, simply notice this.

Partner option

Invite another person to do an experiment with you. Notice the difference it makes if, while you're speaking, someone's face looks back at yours instead of looking at a phone, computer, or TV screen.

Set a timer for two minutes and have a conversation while one of you looks at a phone screen and the other does not. Then switch places. After you've each taken a turn, place your screens away and set a timer for another two minutes, noticing how this feels different.

In each scenario, what do you notice about the other person's face? What do you notice about your own face?

What happens in your body when both of you are present with each other? How does this feel different from when one of you is distracted?

reflection questions

Prompts for Individual Contemplation and Group Discussion

Although you could certainly come up with one- to five-word answers for each question below and move through them quickly, I encourage you to take your time with these, following a rhythm such as the one outlined below. If possible, I encourage you to work through them with another person or a group.

1. Before starting to review the questions, take three deep breaths.
2. If you're in a group, have someone read each question aloud. After hearing or reading the question, hold silence for thirty to sixty seconds to create space to notice what's happening inside and connect your internal stirrings with your thinking brain.
3. Notice what is happening in your body. For example, when answering a question about roadblocks that keep you from connecting with your body, you might sense a tightness in your gut. This might prompt you to reflect, *Just reading this question, I have a tightness in my gut. It doesn't feel good. I want to push past the question and not really feel this. I think I feel nervous, like I might not get this right, or I might stumble across something I don't want to feel, and it just feels a bit risky to explore.*
4. If you're in a group, allow space for responses from different perspectives each of you might hold inside. Resonate and join in the

bliss of saying "Yes!" or "Same!" when you feel what another is expressing. At the same time, honor and explore curiosity with the things you can't resonate with and don't understand. Instead of trying to fix people or correct them, consider asking questions or expressing statements like these:

"I hear you saying _______. Would you be comfortable sharing more about that? I'd like to understand your experience better."

"What is that like? I'd love to better understand what happens in your internal world."

"Thank you for letting us witness ________."

"Thank you for sharing that part of you with us."

Chapter 1

1. What is your gut reaction to the idea of *knowing* something in your body in contrast to *knowing* something in your thinking brain?
2. What kinds of thoughts or reactions happen inside when you let yourself sit with this idea of your body knowing things?
3. In what ways does the idea of *parts* making up the whole of you feel natural, strange, or a mixture of the two?
4. What are your associations with play?
5. Do you feel permission to play with new ideas or practices? If not, what do you sense prevents you from doing so?

Chapter 2

1. What about the idea of slowing down feels enticing?
2. What about the idea of slowing down feels unappealing?

3. What in your life stands most in the way of you slowing down?
4. What do you fear might happen if you moved through life at a slower pace?
5. What beliefs about slowing down have you been taught (e.g., don't be slow or lazy)?
6. What cultural influences most impact how difficult it is to move more slowly through life?

Chapter 3

1. What roadblocks stand in the way of your feeling comfortable connecting with your body?
2. What are the most difficult emotions for you to feel in your body?
3. What fears come up when you consider being more connected to your body?
4. What stands out to you about the psalmists' body-connected language?
5. What messages have you received about your body?
6. What messages about your body popped up while you were reading this chapter?

Chapter 4

1. When you think about the story of the kitten crying in a dark room, how does that feel relatable to or disconnected from the stirrings that live inside you?
2. In what ways does it feels risky to explore the parts of you that are metaphorically shut in a dark room?
3. Who are the parts of you that you've been told are bad?

4. What have you been told (implicitly or explicitly) to do with the parts of you that are bad?
5. What concerns do you have about viewing these parts of you differently?
6. How do you wish you viewed all parts of you, crying kittens and all?

Chapter 5

1. How do you experience the gas pedal in your body?
2. How do you experience the brake system in your body?
3. What are your favorite ways to speed up and move quickly through life (e.g., going for a run or a bike ride, playing games or sports, dancing)?
4. What are your least favorite ways to speed up and move quickly through life (e.g., rushing to work, working out, going for a run)?
5. What are your favorite ways to slow down (e.g., taking a nap, going to bed, watching a movie, sitting in a park)?
6. What are your least favorite ways to slow down (e.g., being "unproductive," being sick, sitting stuck in traffic)?

Chapter 6

1. How much of your life do you spend in a state of safety?
2. How much of your life do you spend in a state of stress?
3. How much of your life do you spend in a state of shutdown?
4. How do you experience a sense of safety, or a lack of safety, in spiritual spaces?

5. How do you experience stress in spiritual spaces?
6. How do you experience overwhelm in spiritual spaces?

Chapter 7

1. Which protective strategies were most relatable? How do you see yourself and others move through these in life?
2. How do you think the logic and goals of protective strategies shift the way that we engage with others? For example, when a part of us is activated into a fight response, how do we see people and the world around us?
3. What high elevations of stress are you used to climbing?
4. What deep sea depths of overwhelm are you used to drowning in?
5. How do you envision a life that is grounded at sea level, allowing you the flexibility to hike and swim through the stressors of life, while able to connect back to your anchor? What might the literal anchors in your life be that ground you at this baseline?

Chapter 8

1. What feels most difficult about extending curiosity toward yourself?
2. In what ways does it feel easier to extend curiosity toward other people? Why do you think this is?
3. What's an example of a critical reaction that tends to pop up inside of you (e.g., something you say to yourself or think when you feel you've messed something up)? How might a curious approach look different from this reaction?
4. What's an example of a critical reaction you have toward yourself that you would never have toward another person?

5. How does learning a person's story change your perspective?
6. Do you think story is powerful enough to move us from criticism to curiosity? Why or why not?

Chapter 9

1. What toys or pets would you reach for, hold, and pull close as a child?
2. What, if anything, do you reach for, hold, and pull close now as an adult?
3. Who were the people available for you to reach for, hold, and pull close as a child?
4. What has it been like when you have not had someone available to reach for, even though you wished you had?
5. Which of the movements described in the chapter—yield, push, reach, hold, pull—feels riskiest to explore?
6. Which of the movements described in the chapter—yield, push, reach, hold, pull—feels most exciting to explore?

Chapter 10

1. In what ways do you resonate with feeling uneasy about fully yielding into safety?
2. How would you describe your internal dialogue when your body is scanning for threats and won't let you fully rest?
3. What feels most risky about fully sinking into safety? Do you feel this generally or specifically (e.g., in friendships, romantic relationships, group settings, at work, with family)?
4. What aspects of safety do you most long to savor and embrace?

5. What do you suspect you might need to feel safe enough to take vulnerable risks, internally or externally?

Chapter 11

1. What do you most frequently give your face and presence to each day (e.g., your computer screen, phone, coworkers, family, friends, animals)?
2. Who offers their face and presence most freely to you (e.g., family, friends, coworkers, animals)?
3. Does it feel paradoxical to imagine offering your face and presence to facets of your own being? How comfortable do you feel imagining offering your face and presence to a part of you?

If you would like spiritual integration, continue on with the following questions. If not, continue to the next chapter's reflection questions.

4. What comes to mind when you imagine God's face and presence?
5. Do any parts of you feel overwhelmed or scared by the thought of being in God's presence or experiencing attunement with God's face? If so, which ones?
6. What do you think about the intersection between language used in ancient Hebrew to describe God's face-presence and what neuroscience is teaching us about attunement? How does this change the way you think about connecting with God or about us connecting with others as God's image bearers?

Chapter 12

1. What kinds of movements help you feel most connected to your body?

2. What kinds of movements have you always been interested in but never given yourself permission to explore (e.g., a type of dance, sport, outdoor adventuring, or some form of artistry)?
3. In what ways do you think the intensity of your walks or workouts might express something that is stirring within?
4. How do you think your past experiences shape your idea of what will happen in the future?
5. How easy or difficult is it for you to imagine a hypothetical scenario that you've never experienced happening in the future?
6. If someone you love were a garden that you were tending, how would you care for that garden? How would that look different from when the garden being tended is you?

further exploration

Therapeutic Jargon and Resources

If you are interested in learning more about the therapeutic terminology and concepts addressed in this book, this section is for you! In addition to brief definitions of concepts, you'll find a selection of names of authors and researchers who have written resources on these topics if you would like to continue your exploration.

Autonomic Landscape

Autonomic nervous system: The autonomic nervous system is part of our peripheral nervous system, which regulates unconscious and involuntary bodily functions such as our heart rate, breathing, blood pressure, digestion, and sexual arousal.

Polyvagal theory: Developed by researcher Stephen Porges, polyvagal theory helps us understand how we engage with the world around us when faced with varying degrees of stressors, threats, and safety. Depending on the cues of safety or threat around us, we will move through different autonomic states, termed *ventral vagal*, *sympathetic*, and *dorsal*, as described below.

> *Ventral vagal:* In this state, our body feels safe enough to be at rest. When we are here, we are regulated and most open to connect with those around us.

Sympathetic: When we are in this state, we are fueled for action. This is our body's gas pedal, mobilizing us to move through or away from stressors and threats.

Dorsal: In this state, our system is overwhelmed and we shut down. Instead of being fueled for action, we are immobilized.

Neuroception: The subconscious detection of cues of stressors, threats, or safety in and around us. This term was coined by Stephen Porges.

Vagal brake: The neural mechanism that helps our body speed up or slow down by regulating our heart rate as we respond to what's happening around us and inside us.

For more information about polyvagal theory and the autonomic nervous system, see the many works of psychologist Stephen Porges and clinician Deb Dana.

Parts Work

Part: Therapeutic models often view parts as portions of the personality or the mind. In this book, we have looked at parts as more holistic strands of our being that are not limited to mind or personality but are woven through our body, mind, soul, and more. Parts of us are impacted by our autonomic state and often reside or come to life when we are in specific autonomic states (e.g., one part of us might become rigid and anxious in a state of stress, as opposed to being flexible and playful in a state of safety).

Inner child: A part of us that holds the age, memory, experience, and perspective of a younger version of ourselves.

Integration: The therapeutic work of bringing disconnected parts of ourselves into more cohesive connection.

Fragmentation: The splitting of parts from our core sense of self, specifically as it relates to a survival strategy when we experience trauma.

For books, a flip chart, and a workbook that explore parts of us, specifically in relation to trauma, see the published works of psychologist Janina Fisher. To explore Internal Family Systems theory, see the works of therapist Richard Schwartz. To explore inner child work or shadow work, see the works of psychologist Carl Jung.

Interpersonal Neurobiology

Attachment: An emotional bond that holds together a relationship between a person and another person, animal, or thing.

Attunement: Awareness and responsiveness to another person. When we attune with another, we open ourselves to resonate internally with what is happening inside them, not only being with them, but also feeling with them. When we offer this kind of embodied empathy, we foster connection and a secure sense of attachment with the other person.

For more information about these concepts, see the works of psychiatrist Daniel Siegel and clinical psychologist Sue Johnson.

Satisfaction Cycle

The satisfaction cycle is a set of intuitive developmental movements that we learn in the first years of life. These basic neurological actions progress through a cycle, building on each other, starting and ending with yield. These movements are simpler when we are infants (e.g., pushing into a crawl or reaching for a toy). Each movement continues to hold significance into our adulthood, such as when we reach for a new job or pull a loved one close. Many people have not experienced the necessary support they needed to seamlessly move through this cycle with their caregivers, which can make it difficult to move through this cycle in later relationships. As adults, we can tend to all ages that make up our adult self, offering them whatever kind of safety they might need to explore the cycle of these movements in our present context.

Yield: Surrendering the full weight of our being to gravity—simply being as our muscles relax and release.

Push: Exploring independence, boundaries, and momentum by moving away from a person, place, or thing.

Reach: Seeking out curiosity and connection.

Hold: Taking hold of what we long for or need (also referred to as *grasp*). Note: This movement happens in conjunction with *pull.*

Pull: Bringing close what we long for or need. Note: This movement happens in conjunction with *hold.*

For more information about the movements of *yield*, *push*, *reach*, *hold*, and *pull*, see the work of movement artist, researcher, and therapist Bonnie Bainbridge Cohen.

notes

FOREWORD BY CHUCK DEGROAT

1. Teresa of Ávila, *The Interior Castle*, trans. Mirabai Starr (Riverhead, 2004), 35.

BEFORE YOU BEGIN

1. Our prefrontal cortex—or what I refer to in this book as our thinking brain—is certainly a gift and remarkably capable of managing executive functions. Other areas of our brain include our limbic system, which is deeply connected with emotions and relationships, and our brain stem, which keeps us alive by regulating basic automatic functions like breathing. Each of these works in concert with our entire brain and body—often beneath our conscious awareness.
2. If you would like more details about the clinical terminology and theories behind the chapters, see "Further Exploration: Therapeutic Jargon and Resources" on page 209.
3. Merriam-Webster, "psychology," accessed December 9, 2024, https://www.merriam-webster.com/dictionary/psychology.
4. While dualistic views promoting a separation between body and soul are sometimes associated with Christian traditions, Scripture does not support this as we often assume. My understanding of the soul is informed by scholars such as N. T. Wright, who clarifies that in the New Testament, rather than the soul simply being a part of us, this word instead reflects "underlying Hebrew or Aramaic words referring not to a disembodied entity hidden within the outer shell of the disposable body but rather to what we would call the whole person. . . . In other words, the idea that every human possesses an immortal soul, which is the 'real' part of them, finds little support in the Bible." See *Surprised by Hope* (HarperOne, 2008), 28. When speaking of the depths of the soul, I am therefore referencing the depths of the whole of our being, rather than isolating one part of us or creating an internal division.

5. Since this book is not a resource that looks to interpret or apply passages of Scripture but instead observes a selection of language used by ancient psalmists, the meanings of Hebrew and Greek words that are referenced are sourced from lexicons, dictionaries, and commentaries rather than modern English translations such as the New Living Translation or New International Version. As much as the biblical studies nerd in me wanted to offer a more in-depth study of these words and their surrounding passages, I felt strongly that this would take us down rabbit trails that would keep us in our head, instead of helping us anchor in our body. So, we'll simply consider the most raw meanings of visceral and body-centered language as a unique way to connect with our body and a deeply holistic spirituality.
6. In my work as a therapist, and through personal experiences, I have seen how the language we use to refer to God can become complicatedly intertwined with painful and traumatic experiences. The assumption that God is male, and the use of male pronouns to refer to God, can become especially unhelpful for many. For this reason, along with theological considerations that are informed by Scripture, I do not use male pronouns in reference to God. While there is not space here for me to share all of my thoughts about this, I invite you to take a look at Wheaton College professor Amy Peeler's work *Women and the Gender of God* (Eerdmans, 2022). Along with this, anytime I refer to God and another term like *Love* is a better fit for you for any reason, I invite you to adjust my words to terminology that communicates the most safety for your reading.

CHAPTER 1: SLOWING DOWN TO ANCHOR IN

1. Robert H. Howland, "Vagus Nerve Stimulation," *Current Behavioral Neuroscience Reports* 1, no. 2 (2014): 64–73, https://link.springer.com/article/10.1007/s40473-014-0010-5.
2. The term *vagus nerve* is based on the Latin *vagus*, which means "wandering" since this cranial nerve reaches from our brain all the way down to our large intestine. While much of what we will play with in this book relates to our vagus nerve, we won't use a lot of technical language, which tends to keep us in our head. Instead, stories and prompts will enable us to connect with our gut-level experiences that are related to the vagus nerve in our everyday lives. Since this nerve is connected to our gut-level sense of whether we feel safe or not, we can easily explore what's happening inside in these ways, even if they aren't as head-knowledge focused as an anatomy textbook.

   If you'd like to dive into a technical source that details how information is communicated between our brain and organs beneath our brain—by means of the vagus nerve—see Hans-Rudolf Berthoud and Winfried L. Neuhuber, "Functional Anatomy of Afferent Vagal System," *Autonomic Neuroscience: Basic and Clinical* 85, no. 1 (December 20, 2000): 1–17, https://doi.org/10.1016/S1566-0702(00)00215-0. Note: The direction of signals from the body to brain is described in medical literature as afferent, in contrast with the efferent, which describes signals being sent from the brain to the body. For more accessible resources about the vagus nerve, see the works of Deb Dana and Stephen Porges, who are listed together in the additional resource "Further Exploration: Therapeutic Jargon and Resources" on page 210.

3. A variety of therapeutic approaches utilize some form of parts work, including but not limited to Inner Child work, Shadow Work, and the widely popularized Internal Family Systems theory. My understanding of parts in a therapeutic approach has been shaped most significantly by psychotherapist Janina Fisher, whose trainings and published work include reflections on the intersections between parts of us and the autonomic nervous system. My approach here is not limited to one systematic model of parts work and attempts to offer more open and flexible language to explore and connect with our multifaceted and embodied being.
4. Tuning in with all parts of ourselves can sometimes lead to questions about how this relates to sin and spiritual warfare. Just as a significant part of Christ initiating God's restorative new creation work included spending intimate time with vulnerable and wounded people, our focus in these pages will be tending to the most overlooked, weary, and outcast parts of our created being.
5. Genesis 1:27, 31.
6. Along with many of the prompts in the chapters ahead, these are simply some of my favorite ways to be with emotions and other internal stirrings. None of them are informed by one single therapist or modality, but instead have been shaped by years of personal and professional experiences.

CHAPTER 2: SLOWING DOWN ISN'T SO SIMPLE

1. I was first introduced to the importance and impact of slowing things down in therapeutic work while training in Emotionally Focused Therapy, developed by clinical psychologist Sue Johnson. This was reinforced when I completed Janina Fisher's Certified Clinical Trauma Professional training, which is focused on working with the neurobiological legacy of trauma.
2. Sensing what's happening inside of us is part of a process that's referred to as interoception: the ability to sense and respond to internal cues, such as hunger and thirst, along with emotions. This concept is attributed to Sir Charles S. Sherrington who coined the term in 1906 when he wrote *The Integrative Action of the Nervous System*. While we won't use this clinical terminology, much of our work in this book has to do with interoception, getting in touch with what's happening inside and exploring how we might respond to these cues in new ways.
3. For more on the complex interplay between our body and the stress we carry, see Bessel van der Kolk's *The Body Keeps the Score* (Viking, 2014), Gabor Maté's *When the Body Says No* (Wiley, 2003), and Hillary L. McBride's *The Wisdom of Your Body* (Baker, 2021).

CHAPTER 3: SLOWING DOWN WITH OUR BODY

1. My understanding of how we tune in with the body has been informed clinically by psychotherapist Pat Ogden, creator of Sensorimotor Psychotherapy, who, with coauthor Janina Fisher, surveys how we might tap into and work with the body's innate intelligence in therapeutic work in *Sensorimotor Psychotherapy: Interventions for Trauma and Attachment* (W. W. Norton & Co., 2015).
2. Psalm 55:4.
3. Psalm 16:9.
4. Psalm 102:4.
5. Psalms 7:9; 26:2. Kidneys were "thought to be the seat of conscience as the heart was thought to be the seat of understanding. The two terms are often joined, either in a collocation ('heart and kidneys') or . . . in parallel versets." Robert Alter, *The Hebrew Bible: A Translation with Commentary*, vol. 3, *Writings* (W. W. Norton, 2018), note on Psalm 73:21.
6. Psalm 102:4-7.
7. Psalm 22:14.
8. Psalm 42:5, 11.
9. Psalms 22:1; 32:3; 38:8.
10. Psalm 39:3.
11. Psalm 77:4.
12. Psalm 55:2, 5.
13. Psalm 38:6-10.
14. Psalms 25:17; 31:9; 38:6, 10.
15. Psalms 16:9; 57:7.
16. Psalm 63:5.
17. Psalm 131:2.

CHAPTER 4: SLOWING DOWN TO LISTEN IN

1. Psalms 10:1; 44:24.
2. In working with ancient texts, my training in hermeneutics and conceptualization of assumptions is largely influenced by Hans-Georg Gadamer's book *Truth and Method.* My first introduction to exploring assumptions in a clinical setting was based on the work of Aaron Beck and Cognitive Behavioral Therapy. My understanding of assumptions we carry in our body was further informed by working with beliefs in other modalities such as Eye Movement Desensitization and Reprocessing (EMDR), developed by Francine Shapiro.
3. For an accessible discussion of these Hebrew words from biblical scholars Carissa Quinn and Tim Mackie, see *The Bible Project* podcast episode "The Womb of God?," August 31, 2020, https://bibleproject.com/podcast/the-womb-of-god/. For technical notes on this Hebrew word, see רחם OT.1.(b) in Willem A. VanGemeren, *New International Dictionary of Old Testament Theology and Exegesis* (Zondervan, 1997); and רחם I.1 in G. Johannes Botterweck, Helmer Ringgren, and Heinz-Josef Fabry, ed., *Theological Dictionary of the Old Testament* (Eerdmans, 2003).

4. Matthew 9:36; 14:14; 15:32; 18:27; 20:34; Mark 1:41; 6:34; 8:2; Luke 7:13. For the meaning of this Greek word, see Frederick William Danker, ed., *BDAG: A Greek–English Lexicon of the New Testament and Other Early Christian Literature*, 3rd edition (University of Chicago Press, 2000).
5. Genesis 1:27, 31.

CHAPTER 5: TUNING IN WITH INTERNAL MOVEMENTS

1. My references to an internal gas pedal and brake system are simplified from the work of Stephen Porges. For more, see *The Polyvagal Theory: Neurophysiological Foundations of Emotions, Attachment, Communication, and Self-Regulation* (W. W. Norton, 2011).
2. Porges, *The Polyvagal Theory*, 11–19.
3. Clinician Deb Dana uses this analogy when talking about the vagal brake. She is widely recognized as a translator of Porges's work on polyvagal theory, making concepts from his work more accessible to clinicians and clients.

CHAPTER 6: TUNING IN WITH INTERNAL STATES

1. The way I visually map out these three states of our autonomic nervous system has been most influenced by a graphic created by Sarah Schlote. For the most updated version of her visual at the time of this book's publication, see https://www.equusoma.com/wp-content/uploads/2020/04/Polyvagal-Defense-Hierarchy-A4.pdf.
2. These three categories are based on the work of Stephen Porges, author of *The Polyvagal Theory: Neurophysiological Foundations of Emotions, Attachment, Communication, and Self-Regulation* (W. W. Norton, 2011), 158–161. In his book, these states are described as ventral vagal, sympathetic, and dorsal. When I use the terminology of safety, stress, and shutdown, my understanding of these states is informed by Porges's work.
3. Porges, *The Polyvagal Theory*, 16, 160.
4. Deb Dana, *Anchored: How to Befriend Your Nervous System Using Polyvagal Theory* (Sounds True, 2021), image 8.1 "Stretched-to-Stress Continuum," 108.
5. Psalm 55:2, 4.
6. Psalm 38:6-10.
7. Psalms 57:7; 63:5.
8. If you follow the work of Deb Dana or simply prefer the autonomic ladder that lists these three states in reverse order, feel full freedom to list each state in whichever order works best for you! Since I focus a lot of my work on anchoring in safety, I like to place safety at the bottom of visual representations of these states.

CHAPTER 7: TUNING IN WITH INTERNAL REACTIONS

1. My understanding of these protective strategies is influenced by the work of psychotherapist Janina Fisher. While I deviate from some of her terminology, the concepts in this section are still informed by her work. For a helpful overview

of Fisher's therapeutic approach and the research that informs it, see *Healing the Fragmented Selves of Trauma Survivors: Overcoming Internal Self-Alienation* (Routledge, 2017).

2. My understanding of parts of us being activated by our autonomic state is informed by the work of psychotherapist Janina Fisher.
3. Janina Fisher refers to this kind of part as a "cry for help" or "attach" part.
4. Countless books and articles use various alliterations to describe fight, flight, freeze, and beyond. Some include additional vocabulary such as *feign* death and *faint*, or they don't include the full list included here. As you explore these categories in this book and other resources, more than trying to learn the "correct" terminology, see what it's like to look for language that most resonates with your experience of protective strategies.
5. This analogy organizes the three autonomic states posited by polyvagal theory in an order that is modeled after the states of autonomic arousal suggested in the window of tolerance, developed by Daniel J. Siegel, clinical professor of psychiatry at UCLA. While polyvagal theory and the window of tolerance are not precisely synonymous, their similarities provide helpful ways to conceptualize and categorize our somatic experiences of feeling calm or distressed.

CHAPTER 8: TUNING IN WITH INTERNAL STORIES

1. A number of therapeutic approaches work with the idea of an inner critic or internal judgmental voice. Psychologists Hal and Sidra Stone began using the specific term *inner critic* in their work in the 1970s.
2. A comprehensive set of more extensive reflections for each chapter of this book is provided in an additional resource on pages 179–191.
3. My approach to consider how seemingly problematic parts of us might be trying to help us is informed by the work of Janina Fisher, who integrates a number of therapeutic approaches, including the Internal Family Systems theory developed by Richard Schwartz.
4. Emotionally Focused Therapy, an evidenced-based approach to couples counseling developed by clinical psychologist Sue Johnson, conceptualizes the patterns we get stuck in with our partners, referring to them as negative cycles. For more, see Sue Johnson, *Hold Me Tight: Seven Conversations for a Lifetime of Love* (Little, Brown and Co., 2008).

CHAPTER 9: TENDING TO WHAT'S BEEN FORGOTTEN

1. These concepts come from the work of movement artist, researcher, and therapist Bonnie Bainbridge Cohen. In her work, she emphasizes both the importance of these movements in our early developmental years, and ways we can feel stuck and find healing in relation to these movements across our lifespan. My integration of how our internal gas pedal and brake system interact with these movements is (to my knowledge) original.

CHAPTER 10: TENDING TO WHAT'S BEEN WOUNDED

1. The way I explore the complexities of vulnerability and safety is informed by the work of Stephen Porges and his colleague Deb Dana, two cofounders of the Polyvagal Institute. Stephen Porges is quoted as having said, "If you want to improve the world, start by making people feel safer."
2. This well-known phrase was coined by Canadian neuropsychologist Donald Hebb.

CHAPTER 11: TENDING TO HIDDEN LONGINGS

1. How we offer our presence and attunement to others is helpfully explored in an interdisciplinary field of study called interpersonal neurobiology (IPNB) developed by Daniel J. Siegel. Here, we'll be considering how these principles can be applied to tuning in with and tending toward parts of ourselves, along with the ways that God and others might engage with parts of us, and vice versa.
2. Psalms 10:1, 11; 13:1; 22:1; 30:7; 44:24; 69:17; 88:14; 102:2; 143:7.
3. Psalms 22:11, 24; 27:8; 31:16; 67:1; 80:3, 7, 19; 89:15; 119:135.
4. Psalms 10:17; 17:6; 31:2; 40:1; 45:10; 49:4; 71:2; 78:1; 86:1; 88:2; 102:2; 116:2; 119:36, 149; 141:4.
5. The suggestion for this translation was made by Dr. Christine Palmer, whose course in Hebrew exegesis I took at Gordon-Conwell Theological Seminary. She holds a PhD in Bible and the Ancient Near East from Hebrew Union College.
6. This exercise is an adaption of sand tray therapy developed by psychiatrist Margaret Lowenfeld.

CHAPTER 12: TENDING TO NEW MOVEMENTS

1. This therapeutic intervention is based on the work and teaching of psychotherapist Janina Fisher.
2. Stephen Porges uses the term *hybrid state* in *Polyvagal Theory: Neurophysiological Foundations of Emotions, Attachment, Communication, and Self-Regulation* (W. W. Norton, 2011), 278.
3. The foundations for how I understand mindful movement are influenced by Pat Ogden and Janina Fisher. For more, see their book, *Sensorimotor Psychotherapy—Interventions for Trauma and Attachment* (W. W. Norton & Co., 2015).
4. Clinical training by Janina Fisher first informed my thinking about imagining new ways to care for parts of us. My understanding of this was recently reinforced in new ways when reading *The Deepest Place: Suffering and the Formation of Hope* (Zondervan, 2023) by Curt Thompson. In this book, Thompson emphasizes how we tell stories of our past in ways that shape our future. He also explores the power of experiencing something different to imagine something new.
5. A number of therapeutic modalities utilize some form of what is often termed *active imagination*, which was developed by Carl Jung.

6. The idea of not blaming a withering leaf for not taking care of itself is based on a poem by Stephanie Cheryl, a dear friend. The lines I derived this imagery from read:

   we've never said to the dying plant,
   "look at this disease. look at these dead leaves. you are bad. you are broken. you did this to yourself."
   no,
   we look at her and say,
   "oh, I'm so sorry. you must not have had enough sunlight, enough water, enough music, enough dancing, enough holding, enough care."
   we are the diseased, the dead leaves, the sunlight, the water, the music, the dancing, the holding, the care.
   we watch with wonder as the diseased leaves, the dead leaves, our leaves come back to life.
   her heartbeat matches mine.
   we have always known how to do this.

   The last line—"we have always known how to do this"—is a quote from words I spoke at a retreat Stephanie and I attended together as I expressed awe at the ways this group of women was caring for each other so beautifully. I hope you take these words with you as you tap into and reconnect with the care of your whole being, something I believe we don't learn how to do but, instead, is something we already know how to do, oftentimes more than we realize.

ADDITIONAL RESOURCES: STRINGING IT ALL TOGETHER

1. These questions are based on the miracle question, an intervention used in Solution Focused therapy. The question was originally developed by Steve de Shazer, Insoo Kim Berg, and their colleagues.

about the author

Anna Christine (A. C.) Seiple is a licensed counselor, retreat leader, instructor, and researcher. She loves integrating neuroscience with spirituality, honoring the entirety of our created being in therapeutic work. Her favorite space for therapy and retreats is outdoors, grounding healing work in movement. She holds two master's degrees—one in clinical mental health counseling and one in biblical studies—and she spent time in a spiritual formation fellowship during her graduate studies. A. C. is currently a postgraduate researcher working on her PhD at the University of St Andrews in Scotland, exploring conversations between ancient Christian contemplation and present-day therapeutic interventions.

Whether she is teaching in a university classroom or a dance studio, she enjoys coming alongside others and finding new ways to continue her own lifelong learning. While A. C. loves to learn in academic settings, her greatest teacher has been painful paths of trauma and loss that have shaped her perspective and longing to cultivate safe and meaningful spaces for others to move through, and with, the trauma and loss they have experienced. When she's not researching or writing, A. C. is soaking up time outdoors, moving freely in a dance class, or going on an adventure with her husband. She loves good food, a good laugh, quality time with friends and family, and finding ways to playfully move through life each day. Connect with A. C. on Instagram @a.c.seiple and find her writing and guided meditations on acseiple.com.